YAHWEH:
Shepherd of the people

Elena Bosetti

YAHWEH
Shepherd of the people

Pastoral symbolism in the Old Testament

ST PAULS

Original title: *La Tenda e il Bastone*
© Edizioni Paoline s.r.l., Cinisello Balsamo, Italy, 1992

Translated from the Italian by *Gina La Spina*
Illustrations by *Giancarlo Gellona & Titta Papandrea*

ST PAULS
Middlegreen, Slough SL3 6BT, United Kingdom
Moyglare Road, Maynooth, Co. Kildare, Ireland

English translation © ST PAULS 1993
ISBN 085439 441 9
Printed in the EEC by Biddles, Guildford

ST PAULS is an activity of the priests and brothers of the
Society of St Paul who proclaim the Gospel through the
media of social communication.

To the young generation

Things that we have heard and known,
that our fathers have told us,
we will not hide from their children,
but tell to the coming generation:
the glorious deeds of the Lord, and his might,
and the wonders which he has wrought
(Ps 78:3-4).

CONTENTS

PREFACE

W hen Abraham rolled up his tent and set off towards an unknown land trusting only in God, he was tracing a symbolic path for all future generations of believers.

For some time now, I have been reflecting on the pastoral symbolism of the Bible. One question came frequently to my mind: what does Israel experience in its nomadic and alien lifestyle when God reveals himself as shepherd? How does Israel reinterpret and live out that experience? Why is this pastoral symbolism so powerful that it continues to be used thousands of years later, even in a society so advanced in technology that such symbolism would seem to be meaningless?

In order to reply adequately, I will trace the socio-cultural horizon within which the pastoral imagery was formed, giving highlights and depth of background to its many different dimensions.

We shall journey through the Old Testament and the Jewish tradition. In the first part, I will present three couples, male and female, who are able to illustrate the richness of reciprocity within the context of the pastoral image. In the second part, I will show how these people and the symbolism of the staff and the tent have constantly inspired the message of the prophets, the prayer of Israel, and in some ways also, the reflections of the sages.

In recent years, various studies have been published presenting the women of the Bible or giving an interpretation of Scripture from the feminist point of view. These works are praiseworthy and important. However, my intention is different and aims to illustrate the reciprocity of women and men in relation to the ongoing history of salvation of the people of God. In fact, the concept of pastoral care as it has emerged from the Second Vatican Council, concerns the entire Christian community, gifted with numerous charisms, and called to give renewed and vigorous expression of its fidelity to the Gospel.

On the other hand, in the Bible the image of the shepherd illustrates the rôle of the one who is placed in authority, and in the tradition of the Churches – both Catholic and Protestant – the title of 'pastor' designates the ordained ministers. Even the Synod of the Roman Catholic Bishops of 1990 on the formation of priests has used the image of the shepherd to describe their spirituality and specific ministry.

While this traditional language shows how much the Church has retained the biblical image, it runs the risk of over-use and ends up being an anachronism. Today pastoral care is spoken of as a reality which has little to do with the biblical image of the shepherd, with the result that its original significance is usually lost. In this context, a deeper understanding of the biblical roots appears relevant in order to renew the pastoral praxis and spirituality.

We shall read the scriptural text in its final redaction as the Church has received it, notwithstanding the problem it occasionally presents to the modern reader.

I will present the text in narrative form, seeking to draw out the complex developments and the various implications of the pastoral symbolism. To this end, I lay precious store on the contribution of the fathers of Israel, who drew their nurture from the Torah. Since, they lived in a similar cultural environment, they were able to perceive the connections and the expressive force of the images throughout the biblical revelation.

In a second volume, I shall explore the symbolism of the shepherd in the New Testament and Christian tradition.

I wish to thank my friend Alviero Niccacci who has offered me valuable suggestions, above all for the interpretation of Micah, Ecclesiastes and the Song of Songs.

I dedicate these pages to the young generations, engaged in the various expressions of pastoral care, with the hope that the Word of God inspires them to work with ever greater wisdom and courage.

THE PASTORAL SYMBOLISM

The image of the shepherd runs through the whole of Scripture from Genesis to the Revelation of St John. It is one of the most precious images in biblical spirituality, rich in attractiveness and warmth, with no hint of a merely languid or romantic interpretation.

The fathers and mothers of Israel, Abraham and Sarah, Isaac and Rebecca, Jacob, Leah and Rachel, were shepherds of small animals (sheep and goats). Taught by their own experience, they understood that God acted in their regard like a good shepherd – vigilant, attentive and caring.

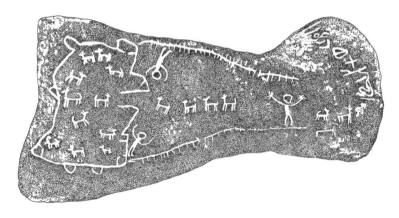

1. HE WILL BE OUR GUIDE
FOR EVER (Ps 48:14)

*Safaita graffito from Amman,
Jordan (VI century BC).*

Thus the image of the shepherd describes the behaviour of God, his 'taking care' of humanity. God loves his people, he guides them, he nurtures them, he defends them, he becomes their companion on the journey.

On this religious foundation, which at the same time is sociological and cultural, there is added a unique experience – that of the exodus. In the seemingly endless wandering towards the promised land – the 40 years in the desert – Israel experiences in a most particular way the closeness of the shepherd-god. It is he who guides them by the hand of Moses, who nurtures and

11

defends them. He is a God who becomes involved with them, who provides, sets his people free, and binds himself in covenant to them.

For this reason, Israel can sing with confidence the psalm, "The Lord is my shepherd, I shall not want" (Ps 23:1). Scripture attributes this psalm to David, the poet-king and player of the harp who pastured his father's sheep on the outskirts of Bethlehem. God chose him, although he was the youngest of his brothers, consecrated him by the hand of the prophet Samuel, and placed him as leader to 'pastor Israel'.

The prophets drew inspiration from David to describe the Messiah, and this figure is seen to be fulfilled in Jesus, the shepherd full of compassion who searches for the lost sheep of Israel and gives his life for all.

Roots in the ancient Near East

The theme of the shepherd, so precious in Scripture, has its roots in a broader cultural context embracing the entire region of the ancient Near East.

Since the third millennium BC, both in Mesopotamia and in Egypt, God was referred to as a shepherd. In Mesopotamia, this title was initially the prerogative of a king, then of the divinity. In Egypt, it is noted that the process is reversed: it is foremost God who is named as shepherd.

Since the pyramids

The most ancient documents that refer to the deity in the image of the shepherd date back to the *Texts of the pyramids* (2500-2250 BC). They are formulae of protection for the deceased sovereign. The Egyptians maintained that after his death the king became immortal and was admitted to the flock of Mekhenty-irty, the blind god who watches over the stars of the night.

In one of these formulae, Mekhenty-irty is described as he who lets the deceased sleep in his arms, therefore in safekeeping, and is called the shepherd of the Pharaoh:

> Behold, he has arrived!
> Behold, he has arrived!
> Behold, your brother has arrived!
> Behold, Mekhenty-irty has arrived!
> Even though you may not recognize him
> You sleep in his embrace.
> Even when your secretion dries up,
> He is as your calf, as your Shepherd (Pyr 1864a-1865b).

As in this text, so in others of the pyramids, the pastoral action of the god is limited to the Pharaoh, and consists in the guarantee of his immortality. One thing, however, is already clear: the shepherd is the one who gives and preserves life in time and in eternity.

Shamash is my shepherd

The *Texts of the pyramids* bear the stamp of aristocracy and are meant almost exclusively for the Pharaoh with some probable exception for the noble classes. However, those who cannot afford to construct tombs for themselves cannot lay claim to immortality. They cannot expect to be led to the shepherd-god in the heavenly pastures.

2. THE LORD IS MY SHEPHERD (Ps 23:1)

Statue in plaster from Mari, Syria (II millennium BC; Aleppo, National Museum).

By contrast, in Mesopotamia the image of the shepherd-god seems to possess a democratic dimension right from the beginning. In fact, we meet expressions of this type: 'Shamash-re'ua'; 'Ir-a-ni-Marduk', which signify: Shamash is my shepherd; Marduk has pastured me. These expressions refer to the individual; they confess that Shamash or Marduk has taken care of a person. In the Mesopotamian concept, success in people's lives does not depend on intelligence or astuteness, nor on heredity, but on the fact that God takes care of them. When they have their God with them, they have everything they need for living: health, well-being, progeny, etc.

From this point of view are interpreted such phrases as:

> The God of man is a shepherd who searches out
> good pastures for man (Vorlander, 70 nr 96).

The Mesopotamian concept of the shepherd-god does not concern itself primarily with life after death, but rather with life here and now. Of a similar meaning are the letters addressed to one's own God to invoke his protection. In one of these, the king Gudea laments not having a personal God:

> Thus speaks Gudea:
> as a sheep I have no shepherd worthy of trust,
> no trustworthy shepherd takes care of me (...)
> My God, I am not your enemy, turn your heart towards me!
>
> (Vorlander, 91-92 nr 140).

Shepherd for all people

A certain democratization of the theology of the shepherd is noticeable in Egypt at the beginning of the First Intermediate Period (2135-2040 BC). It was a period of crisis and instability. The age of the pyramids, the pomp and security of the Ancient Empire give way to unrest, rebellion and the demand for social justice. And it is precisely in this context that the notion of God as shepherd assumes a symbolic value. It serves to express the attitude of the divinity towards creatures, towards all humanity, not only those who are princes and masters.

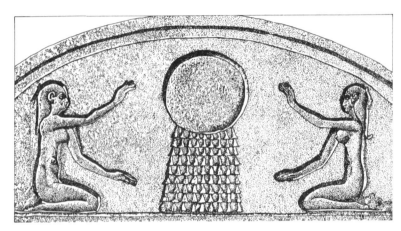

3. YOU RENEW THE FACE OF THE EARTH (Ps 104:30)

Cover of an Egyptian sarcophagus, in granite, of the Tolemaic period from Saqqara, Egypt (III-II century BC; Vienna, Kunsthistorisches Museum).

In a piece of wisdom literature entitled 'Teaching for Merikare', we find the affirmation that people are 'the flock of God'. The king must provide for the people, considering himself not as master but as the representative of God who loves everyone and labours for them:

Provide for the people who are the flock of God.
It is for love of men that he has made the heavens and the earth,
and has contained the greed of the waters.
It is on account of their noses that he has made the wind,
because they are his likeness, come out of his body.
It is for love of them that he rises in the heavens,
for them he made the herbs, the animals,
the birds, and the fish to satisfy their hunger
(Pap. Petersburg 1116A, XI, 9.10; XIII, 3).

Hymns to the sun-god

In more recent ages in the ancient Near East, the image of the shepherd is developed in a theological dimension in the hymns to the sun-god. These are found both in Mesopotamia and in

Egypt, and in them the theology of the shepherd in the ancient non-biblical Near East reaches the peak of its development.

A masterpiece of Mesopotamian literature is the hymn to Shamash (the sun-god), composed towards the end of the second millennium BC, and about 200 verses long. In the first 20 verses, Shamash is exalted because he dispenses light upon all the universe. Following this, he is praised for the care and interest he manifests towards all creatures and he is called 'shepherd':

> You are concerned for peoples of all nations,
> all that Ea, the king, has created has been totally entrusted to you.
> You give pasture to all beings gifted with a living spirit;
> you are their shepherd, be they high or low (...)
> The shepherd of the nether world,
> the shepherd of the world above,
> he who regulates the light of the universe,
> O Shamash, are you! (Seux, 53-54).

The religion of the sun-god is imbued with the sense of universality. In fact, the sun is there for all, it exists for the peoples of all nations. It is not like certain gods who act on behalf of one people to the ruin of others. The sun does not lend itself to the instrumentality of nationalism: he "gives pasture to all beings gifted with a living spirit" wherever they are to be found. It is therefore providence for all and care extended to the whole of creation.

In Egypt the art of el-Amarna, inspired by the religious reform introduced by the king Akhenaton (1371-1356), is most effective in expressing the providence of God. It depicts the rays of the sun ending in the shape of a hand. The rays of the god Aton (the sun disk) are warm, open hands that awaken all things already in existence, and that open the way of life to all that is still to come into being.

The most important document, however, is the hymn of the Egyptian poet Merysekhmet. The sun is acclaimed as the good shepherd of humanity: a shepherd who loves his flock, exercises compassion and knows how to be a shepherd.

These are some of the more significant passages:

> Praise to thee, Amon-Re-Atum-Har-akhti,
> who spoke with his mouth and there came into existence all men,
> gods, large and small cattle in their entirety,
> and that which flies and lights totally (...)
> Thou art valiant *as a herdsman tending them* for ever and ever.
> Bodies are filled with thy beauty; eyes see through (thee).
> The [fear] of thee is for everybody;
> their hearts turn about to thee, good at all times.

4. THE LORD IS GOOD
   (Ps 103:8)

Egyptian limestone sculpture in relief from the temple of Pharaoh Amenofi IV (1367-1350 BC) from el-'Amarnah, Egypt.

Everybody lives through the sight of thee.
Do (not) widows say, "Our husband art thou,"
and little ones, "Our father and our mother"?
The rich boast of thy beauty,
and the poor (worship) thy face.
He that is imprisoned turns about to thee,
and he that has a sickness calls out to thee (...)
Everybody is turned back to thy presence,
so that they may make prayers to thee.
Thy ears are open, hearing them and taking care of them,
O our Ptah who loves his crafts, *herdsman who loves his herds.*
His reward is a goodly burial for the heart which is satisfied with
    truth (...)
How beautiful art thou as a god, O Amon, verily Har-akhti,
a marvel sailing in the heavens
and conducting the mysteries of the underworld!
The gods are coming before thee,
exalting the forms which thou hast assumed.
Mayest thou appear (again) from the hands of Nun,
thou being mysterious in the form of Khepri,
reaching the gates of Nut, beautiful in thy body (...)
How beautiful is thy rising on the horizon!
(Thus) we are in a renewal of life.
We had entered (into) Nun, and it has refreshed (us),
as when one began youth.
The old state has been taken off, another has been put on.
We praise the beauty of thy face (ANET 371-372).

The shepherd-god is capable: he knows how to give and sustain life. He is not indolent. He watches over the flock unceasingly. He loves his work and labours for all, for rich and poor: widows can call him 'husband' and orphans 'father'. He is a God who listens and is moved to compassion.

The shepherd-god is also the one who awakens all things into existence. He lays open the way to life and traces the path. He knows how to be a shepherd! Be it in this world or the next, the life of the believer is in the hands of a good and trustworthy God.

The biblical horizon

As we can see, the Bible is not the first to refer to God in the image of shepherd, but in it the image is imbued with the particular relationship which binds Yahweh to his people. A beautiful example is found in the story of Jacob where for the first time in Scripture, God is called 'my shepherd'. It is not by mere chance that the old patriarch formulates this expression in the land of Egypt, thinking back especially to the journey and the period of his dwelling in Mesopotamia.

Thus a link is ideally drawn between two localities where the theological use of the term 'shepherd' already had a long history. But Jacob adds to it something new and personal. The shepherd-god of his life has no connection with the sun-god that illumined and enlivened all things while remaining above high in the heavens. His shepherd is a God who descends towards man and becomes his companion on the journey.

Flung like a bridge between Mesopotamia and Egypt, Israel emerges from both carrying away treasures of their marvellous culture (Ex 12:35-36; Is 40:10). But these treasures have been re-worked and personalized in biblical literature.

5. IN THE IMAGE OF GOD HE CREATED THEM; MALE AND FEMALE (Gen 1:27)

Bronze statuette from Ascalon, Israel (II millennium BC; Paris, Louvre Museum).

Three key couples

To discover the manner in which Israel has appropriated the pastoral symbolism, we shall refer to six personalities which form three important couples. The first and third couple are husband and wife: Jacob and Rachel; David and Abigail, while the second are brother and sister: Moses and Miriam.

Historically, these persons were all shepherds and they also became so at the symbolic level because of their specific rôle towards the people. The Jewish-biblical tradition (and later the Christian one) has stressed this symbolic value, presenting these figures as models for the leaders of the people.

The first couple fulfils the pastoral symbolism in terms of fatherhood and motherhood. Jacob and Rachel are not merely tribal ancestors of the people, but father and mother in the faith.

Moses and Miriam personify the pastoral symbolism above all as prophecy and deliverance. Through their mediation, God led Israel out of Egypt and brought them together at Sinai, the place of revelation and covenant.

Finally, David and Abigail symbolize the royal dimension. David is the shepherd who becomes king and Abigail the shepherdess who saves him from interpreting his new rôle in terms of might and arrogance, substituting his judgement for the justice of God.

The tent and the staff

The three couples that we are going to explore are marked by a fundamental symbolism derived from the ancient nomadic way of life.

For the modern reader a word of explanation may be necessary. In the Bible, as in the other civilizations of the ancient

Near East, the life of the nomad was regarded in a manner far removed from what appears to our modern eyes. It was the condition that permitted entire tribes and populations to survive, moving from one place to another according to climatic variations (rainy seasons), or to deal with famine (see the descent of the Hebrews into Egypt). This dimension of mobility and itinerancy that particularly characterizes the life of the shepherd was in no way regarded as a negative experience. On the contrary, the bedouins felt proud of their liberty. Unlike sedentary people who were obliged to put down roots in their locality like the plants, the bedouins were not bound to any place (while retaining points of reference such as springs and wells) and on this account, they felt extremely proud, like those who hold their destiny in their own hands. Their houses were tents, dwellings which were both light and portable. They could be erected wherever the bedouins thought best, and they presented the bedouins with no obstacles to resuming their journey.

6. ENLARGE THE SPACE OF YOUR TENT (Is 54:2)
Bedouin tent.

From the social point of view the tent is the place which eminently facilitates the bonding of the family group and the welcoming of guests. The God of Israel who participates in the journeying of his people shares their dwelling under the tent. This expresses on the one hand, the bonds of kinship which Yahweh contracted with Israel by virtue of the covenant, and on the other, the fact that Israel found refuge and hospitality in the tent of Yahweh. In fact, to enter within the tent signifies the right of asylum. The host is a person who is sacred and inviolable.

Israel experiences this in the face of their enemies. Their enemies strive to overcome them but are obliged to come to a halt 'outside', powerless to enter. Yet, Israel is received and welcomed into the tent of Yahweh and enjoys his ineffable hospitality: perfumed oil is poured on the head, the cup over-flows with wine (see Psalm 23).

But the tent is not pitched for stability, it is made to be shifted. The flexibility of its structure permits the enlargement of its dimension on the basis of the number in the clan, and the movement from one location to another according to the needs determined by the nomadic lifestyle. Similarly, the wonderful presence of God (*shekinah*) has placed his tent in Israel in a form which permits the widening and moving on. In the tent of the God of Israel, a welcome awaits even the pagans, the nations of all the earth:

> Enlarge the place of your tent, and let the curtains of your habitations be stretched out; hold not back, lengthen your cords and strengthen your stakes. For you will spread abroad to the right and to the left, and your descendants will possess the nations and will people the desolate cities (Is 54:2-3).

To achieve this capacity for openness and hospitality, it is necessary to advance, to remove the tent from acquired posi-tions and embark on a journey towards a new encampment.

Israel is a people on the march. They are not in search of adventure or conquest, without any definite goal, but rather they are a people on a pilgrimage towards the promised land. The staff is a reminder of the road that stretches ahead of them and is used resolutely to quicken the pace and to defend them-selves from the dangers on the journey.

Staff and tent go together. One gives rhythm to the journey, the other ease and comfort in the resting place. The tent and the staff link symbolically the three couples we are illustrating. On the return journey to the promised land, in prayer on the banks of the River Jabbok, Jacob remembers that with his staff alone he had crossed that stream. Now, however, thanks to the divine favour, he "can form two companies" (Gen 32:11). It therefore seems right and proper for him to go to Bethel and erect there an altar to the God who had appeared to him while he was fleeing to save his life.

The biblical account attributes a special significance to the folding up of the tent and moving on to Bethel:

And as they journeyed, a terror from God fell upon the cities that were round about them, so that they did not pursue the sons of Jacob. And Jacob came to Luz (that is, Bethel), which is in the land of Canaan, he and all the people who were with him, and there he built an altar, and called the place El-bethel, because there God had revealed himself to him when he fled from his brother (Gen 35:5-7).

As the name indicates, Bethel is the house of God. An important aspect of Jacob's pastoral rôle is to lead his family to Bethel, in other words, to give testimony to his faith in the God of the promise and pass it on to his children.

The last time Jacob moves his tent is to descend into Egypt. He does so reluctantly despite his desire to see Joseph, the son of Rachel again. But the conviction that never leaves him in the descent, as in the return from Egypt (the exodus), is that all is under the guidance of the divine shepherd (Gen 46:1-4). In this way, the staff of Jacob gives direction for the tent of his sons at Bethel and then follows them into a foreign land.

Just as Jacob conducted his sons to Bethel where he had personally encountered the God of Abraham and Isaac, so Moses would lead Israel to Sinai, the mountain on which the God of his fathers revealed himself to him while he was pasturing the sheep of another (Ex 3:1-12). What emerges here is the idea that the pastoral rôle of the father, like that of the prophet and leader, is inseparable from personal experience.

At Sinai, Israel finds again the God of their fathers ("Moses led the people out of the camp to meet God", Ex 19:12), listens to the voice of God and makes a commitment to observe the covenant with Yahweh. The Lord orders a tent to be built that he may dwell in the midst of his people and go before them on the journey. Sinai is not, in fact, the final goal. From there, too, the tent must be pulled up to move on.

On this journey, the leader is seen symbolically by means of the shepherd's staff of Moses, brought to Egypt from the land of Midian. With it, Moses performs the prodigies of the exodus and opens the way for them to return to the promised land.

Staff and tent are also a distinguishing feature in the experience of David. With the shepherd's staff in hand, he confronts the gigantic enemy; subsequently that staff becomes the sign of his royalty (sceptre). The link with the nomadic past is evidenced by the tent where the Lord still dwells while the people have gone on to live sedentary lives in houses of stone.

In conclusion, the symbols of the staff and tent express in an effective manner both the dynamic dimension and utopian nature of biblical pastoral symbolism.

Pastoral care is utopia, in the original sense of the term. It is necessary to move the tent forward from the *topos* (place where it is) to where it has not yet reached (*u-topos*). This was done by the fathers and mothers of Israel – Moses, and Miriam the prophetess who instructs the women and intones the song of deliverance; and this was done by David when, from shepherding the flocks of his father, he was called to govern Israel. The people of God is called to do the same with regard to the nations until the day when the tent of divine love will be home for all.

> Look upon Zion, the city of our appointed feasts! Your eyes will see Jerusalem, a quiet habitation, an immovable tent, whose stakes will never be plucked up, nor will any of its cords be broken. But there the Lord in majesty will be for us a place of broad rivers and streams, where no galley with oars can go, nor stately ship can pass.
> For the Lord is our judge, the Lord is our ruler, the Lord is our king; he will save us.
> Your tackle hangs loose; it cannot hold the mast firm in its place, or keep the sail spread out. Then prey and spoil in abundance will be divided; even the lame will take the prey.
> And no inhabitant will say, "I am sick"; the people who dwell there will be forgiven their iniquity (Is 33:20-24).

The preaching of the prophets and the prayer of Israel are situated within this dynamic and utopian perspective which traces ever-widening horizons for the people of God.

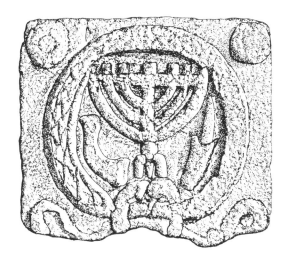

7. HE WILL SAVE US (Is 33:22)

Menorah, Jewish candlestick with seven branches (V century London, British Museum).

21

HISTORY AND STORY

*Men and women
in pastoral imagery*

JACOB AND RACHEL

The first mention of God as shepherd in the Bible is Genesis 48:15. Here the speaker is Jacob, already advanced in years and experience, having descended into Egypt with his sons to survive the famine. The context is a rite of adoption. The venerable patriarch blesses and acknowledges as his own the two sons born in the land of Egypt to Joseph, the firstborn son of Rachel. These are his words:

> And he blessed Joseph, and said, "The God before whom my fathers Abraham and Isaac walked,
> the God who has led me all my life long to this day,
> the angel who has redeemed me from all evil, bless the lads!"
> (Gen 48:15-16).

8. MY SHEPHERD ALL MY LIFE TO THIS DAY (Gen 48:15)

Terracotta statuette from Susa, Iraq (XVIII century BC; Paris, Louvre Museum).

The reader will note that the verses advance slowly and the movement seems almost restrained. Before arriving at the main verb ('bless') there is a whole series of epithets, a concentration on titles referring to the God whose blessing is being invoked. Jacob makes a distinction between his own relationship with God and that of his fathers. Abraham and Isaac have walked before God, according to the formula used for the patriarchs before the flood (so also Enoch: Gen 5:22-24 and Noah: Gen 6:9), but for Jacob, God has been 'shepherd' since the first day of his life.

Not only this, but he calls his God "the angel who has redeemed me from all evil". Although it may sound strange, the angel is none other than Yahweh, or rather a manifestation of him between the invisible and the visible, capable of filling the abyss between the world of God and that of humanity. The figure of the angel, or of some mysterious being, appears many times in the history of the patriarchs. Three persons pay a visit to Abraham (Gen 18), an angel protects the servant of Abraham on his journey (Gen 24:40), various angels meet Jacob at Mahanaim (Gen 32:3) and a mysterious man wrestles with him on the banks of the River Jabbok (Gen 32:25). Again we find this figure in the traditions of the Exodus where we read that the angel of Yahweh accompanied the people in their journeying towards the promised land (Ex 23:20).

But the title that merits the greatest attention in Genesis 48:15 is that of 'shepherd', since Jacob declares that his God had been such for him from his birth until that day, when he was 140 years old. What was the experience underlying this short designation of the God of Jacob? To understand its importance one would need to retrace the story of the patriarch, because it is in the unfolding of his day-to-day existence that Jacob perceived God as a shepherd.

Taken by itself, a title can have little significance. One title could be equivalent to another, and even the most beautiful titles would be not very meaningful. So with the word 'father' there could be the notion of 'master' for one who has undergone the experience of a dominating father figure; and the word 'mother' could also be analogous with 'step-mother'.

Therefore, it is not so much the title of 'shepherd' that we are interested in analysing here, as its significance in the historical context of the nomad Jacob, son of shepherds and himself a shepherd for all of his life.

Let us read the confession of Genesis 48:15 in the light of some key passages in the life-story of the patriarch.

The shepherd is a companion on the journey

The first passage in this overview is Genesis 28:10-22. Jacob is fleeing from his home to safeguard his life, threatened by his brother Esau whose blessing as firstborn son he had usurped. He is heading towards Mesopotamia, the land of his fathers, to arrive at Paddan-Aram in the house of his mother's brother, his uncle Laban. So he actually travelled back the same route of Abraham's exodus (compare Gen 28:10 with Gen 12:4-9).

It is not difficult to imagine the psychological condition of Jacob the fugitive: fear of the brother who plotted to kill him (Gen 27:41); uncertainty, insecurity and anxiety for the many dangers of the journey, but also much hope: after all, the blessing of his father accompanied him! In this situation, charged with fear and hope, God comes to meet him at night during his sleep.

> And he dreamed that there was a ladder set up on the earth, and the top of it reached to heaven; and behold, the angels of God were ascending and descending on it!
> And behold, the Lord stood above it and said, "I am the Lord, the God of Abraham your father and the God of Isaac; the land on

which you lie I will give to you and to your descendants; and your descendants shall be like the dust of the earth, and you shall spread abroad to the west and to the east and to the north and to the south; and by you and your descendants shall all the families of the earth bless themselves" (Gen 28:12-14).

With these words God addresses to Jacob the blessing given to Abraham (see Gen 12:12; 13:14; 15:5 and 22:17-18). Here is a commentary of Rashi, the incomparable medieval master of Hebrew exegesis: "Whatever I promised to Abraham regarding his seed, it was in reference to you that I promised it and not in reference to Esau" (*Commentary* on Gen 28:15).

In particular, God comforts Jacob by declaring himself as his companion on the journey:

> Behold, I am with you and will keep you wherever you go, and will bring you back to this land; for I will not leave you until I have done that of which I have spoken to you (Gen 28:15).

Awakening from sleep, Jacob was seized by wonder and awe:

> Then Jacob awoke from his sleep and said, "Surely the Lord is in this place; and I did not know it" (Gen 28:16).

What he did in the early morning is typical of the manner in which biblical sanctuaries are born and what they properly represent: places which testify to a particular experience of the divine. The sanctuary is built in memory of a 'descent' of God.

> So Jacob rose early in the morning, and he took the stone which he had put under his head and set it up for a pillar and poured oil on the top of it (Gen 28:18).

In the light of this text, the sanctuary is not a place where one goes to ask God to 'come down' in aid of one's needs (as often happens today), but a place that gives witness to the gracious coming of God. It is he who freely descends, comes to meet Jacob, stands above him ("to keep him safe", comments Rashi), commits himself by a promise, and blesses him.

Consequently, the meeting-place becomes a site to remember and a memorial of the event. So Jacob takes the stone he had used as a pillow on that extraordinary night and erects it as a pillar, and consecrates it with oil. He raises it up as a monument, that is, as a memorial to the God who had blessed his life and that of his descendants, and had become personally involved in his existence.

9. HE SET IT UP AS A PILLAR (Gen 28:18)

Stele of basalt from Hazor representing hands raised in prayer (1500 BC; Jerusalem, Museum of Israel).

He called the name of that place Bethel; but the name of the city was Luz at the first (Gen 28:19).

Later, Jacob will return to Bethel and faithfully keep his promise, constructing an altar on this first stone (Gen 35:1).

From promise to wager

God commits himself by a promise and Jacob, who in the Bible is regarded as an astute man, in turn makes a wager precisely on the fidelity of God, "If God will be with me". Note the provocation since God has just said "I am with you and will keep you wherever you go", but he says:

> If God will be with me, and will keep me in this way that I go, and will give me bread to eat and clothing to wear, so that I come again to my father's house in peace, then the Lord shall be my God (Gen 28:20-21).

Herein is the boldness of the biblical man! Here, moreover, is a proof of who Jacob is. He is a fugitive, full of fear, yet he is also the heir of the blessing. God has just assured him, "I will be with you and keep you safe". He has just guaranteed him, "I will give you the land, I will bring you back". Yet, Jacob is not Abraham. He does not appear to be the man who is able to trust unconditionally. True, he erects the pillar as a memorial. But at the same time he wishes to be on the safe side and reasons thus: "Very well, if God goes with me, protects me (he asks only bread to eat and clothes to wear), if he truly brings me home safe and sound, then I will trust him entirely, then God shall be my God. Then, but not before!" And so Jacob transforms the promise into a wager and God plays along with him.

The meeting with Rachel, the beautiful shepherdess

Then Jacob went on his journey, and came to the land of the people of the east (Gen 29:1).

The *Jerusalem Targum* reads in the rapidity of the account (no sooner has Jacob set off than he has arrived) a prodigious event, the fifth accomplished by Jacob after his departure from Beersheba.

> The ground shrivelled before him, and on the same day of his departure he arrived at Haran.

Rashi comments, "As soon as he received the good tidings that he was assured of God's protection his heart lifted up his feet and he walked swiftly" (*Commentary* on Gen 29:1). The biblical text proceeds:

As he looked, he saw a well in the field, and lo, three flocks of sheep lying beside it; for out of that well the flocks were watered. The stone on the well's mouth was large (Gen 29:2).

In the *Midrash Rabbah*, there is a strange interpretation of this scene with the three flocks of sheep crouching close to the well. It sees here an allusion to Moses, Aaron and Miriam:

Because it was at this well that the flocks were watered. Therefore from it each drew forth water for his group, his tribe, his family (Gen R. 70:8).

10. THEY FOUND A WELL OF SPRING WATER (Gen 26:19)

Ancient well in Judea.

The symbolism of the well

What lies behind this interpretation? Is there an intermediate reality that justifies the allegorical leap from the three flocks to the three figures of the exodus?

Yes there is, and it consists of the symbolism of the well as the Law. In the midrashic tradition the well represents the gift of

11. SHE WAS A
SHEPHERDESS (Gen 29:9)

Canaanite divinity (II millennium BC; Paris, Louvre Museum).

the Torah, the life-giving water of the law, divine revelation, and wisdom. The symbolism of the well appears already in the traditions related to Abraham (see Gen 21:22-31 where the patriarch vindicates his claim to the well of Beersheba).

The *Midrash Rabbah* on Genesis 21:31 comments as follows:

> The shepherds of Abraham argued with those of Abimelech and each shouted, the well is ours! Then Abraham's shepherds said, it belongs to those for whom the water will rise when their sheep approach to drink. On seeing the flocks of Abraham the water rose immediately. The Saint, may he be blessed, said to it: You are a sign for your children that the well will rise for them, since it is written. Rise, O well! Sing for him (it) (Gen R. 54:5).

Another targumic tradition lists 'five miracles' performed for Jacob when he left Beersheba (Gen 28:10). The first two refer to the account of Bethel, and the last – which we mentioned previously – to the journey from Bethel to Haran. The third and fourth, however, deal with the symbolism of the well with reference to the scene described in Genesis 29:

> Third miracle: the stone that had to be rolled from the mouth of the well when all the flock had gathered, he rolled it with only one arm.
>
> Fourth miracle: the well overflowed and the water rose up in front of him, and it overflowed every day that he was at Haran (*Jerusalem Targum* on Gen 28:10).

From this well his sons will draw water and in particular the great leaders of the exodus, Moses, Aaron and Miriam. First of all, Rachel, his woman, draws from it:

> While he was still speaking with them, Rachel came with her father's sheep; for she kept them (Gen 29:9).

The text suggests a very beautiful aspect. It is she, Rachel, who stimulates the generous thrust and strength of Jacob:

> Now when Jacob saw Rachel the daughter of Laban his mother's brother, and the sheep of Laban his mother's brother, Jacob went up and rolled the stone from the well's mouth, and watered the flock of Laban his mother's brother (Gen 29:10).

The Jewish tradition has underlined this aspect by playing on two similar roots: *gîl* which means 'to rejoice', and *galah*, meaning 'to uncover, roll away'.

When he saw Rachel his heart rejoicedand he rolled away the
stone with ease (Kasher, 1162).

An analogous explanation appears in another Jewish commentary:

When he saw that Rachel paid attention to his physical strength
he increased his strength and rolled the stone (Kasher, 1162).

It seems important that the meeting between Jacob and Rachel,
the beautiful shepherdess, should take place by the well and
materialize in a service given to her father's sheep. If the well
symbolizes the inexhaustible source of the Torah, the com-
bined presence of Jacob and Rachel recalls the necessary mediation of both man and woman for the water from the well to
actually become accessible to the sheep.

The water is undoubtedly a gracious gift of God. In fact, as
the Jewish account referred to above has it, it rises freely for the
sheep of Abraham and those of his sons. Even so, for this water
to be drinkable, it needs someone to remove the stone from the
well. And this is the joint labour of Jacob and Rachel. On seeing
her, he immediately removes the stone from the well, and the
sheep of her flock are the first to be watered. Only after this is
done, the two embrace and weep.

Rachel, the woman of the heart

Then Laban said to Jacob, "Because you are my kinsman, should
you therefore serve me for nothing? Tell me, what shall your wages
be?"

Now Laban had two daughters; the name of the older was Leah,
and the name of the younger was Rachel.

Leah's eyes were weak, but Rachel was beautiful and lovely.
Jacob loved Rachel; and he said, "I will serve you seven years for
your younger daughter Rachel."

Laban said, "It is better that I give her to you than that I should
give her to any other man; stay with me."

So Jacob served seven years for Rachel, and they seemed to him
but a few days because of the love he had for her (Gen 29:15-20).

The love of Jacob for Rachel is so great that seven years of
service seemed to him only a few days. Rachel was his first and
great love!

Then Jacob said to Laban, "Give me my wife that I may go in to
her, for my time is completed" (Gen 29:21).

Give me my bride! He had deserved her with seven years of

12. HE KISSED RACHEL AND
  WEPT ALOUD (Gen 29:11)

*Egyptian ivory panel decorat-
ing a bed (XVIII-XIX dynasty:
1550-1196 BC; Cairo, Egyptian
Museum).*

voluntary labour, and the desired moment for him to be united with the promised bride was now at hand. But it is here that the artful and cunning Jacob is terribly deceived. He who had withheld by deceit the right of the firstborn from his brother is now himself ironically cheated by his uncle who, in place of Rachel, ushers the older daughter into the marriage chamber:

> And in the morning, behold, it was Leah; and Jacob said to Laban, "What is this you have done to me? Did I not serve with you for Rachel? Why then have you deceived me?" (Gen 29:25).

The *Midrash Rabbah* also makes note of this similarity in the deception presently suffered by Jacob and that previously enacted by him towards his father:

> All night long Jacob called her 'Rachel' and she responded to him. In the morning, however, he discovered it was Lia! Jacob said to Lia, What! you liar and daughter of liars! She replied, Can there be a master without disciples? Did not your father call you Esau and you responded? So, as you called me, I replied! (Gen R. 70:19).

Seeing the deceit, Jacob claims his woman, and in order to have her he promises another seven years of service:

> So Jacob went in to Rachel also, and he loved Rachel more than Leah, and served Laban for another seven years (Gen 29:30).

This passage of Scripture, in a Jewish tradition, is read in the light of the Song of Songs:

> And Jacob loved Rachel. This is what is written:... (Song 8:6), that is, the love with which Jacob loved Rachel, and, as it is written: And Jacob loved Rachel. Steadfast as hell is jealousy, because Rachel was jealous of her sister. And how can love and jealousy abide together?

This question finds an answer in another passage of the midrashic tradition where the attributes of the jealousy and the love of God are paralleled with the jealousy and the love of Rachel. While in some passages Rachel is presented as jealous of her sister, Leah, in others she appears extremely generous, to the extent that her behaviour becomes a model proposed even to God.

Rachel is a woman, so beautiful and desirable, yet who turns out to be sterile. Beautiful, but lacking the capacity to procreate. Her seemingly living tomb is infertile and lifeless. It is the humiliating lot shared by the other wives of the patriarchs such as Sarah (Gen 11:30), Rebekah (Gen 25:21), and now Rachel.

Love and Jealousy

The matriarch Rachel broke forth into speech before the Holy One – blessed be he – and said:

"Sovereign of the universe, it is revealed before thee that thy servant Jacob loved me exceedingly and toiled for my father on my behalf seven years. When those seven years were completed and the time arrived for my marriage with my husband, my father planned to substitute another for me to wed my husband for the sake of my sister.

It was very hard for me, because the plot was known to me and I disclosed it to my husband; and I gave him a sign whereby he could distinguish between me and my sister, so that my father should not be able to make the substitution. After that I relented, suppressed my desire, and had pity upon my sister that she should not be exposed to shame.

In the evening they substituted my sister for me with my husband, and I delivered over to my sister all the signs which I had arranged with my husband so that he should think that she was Rachel. More than that, I went beneath the bed upon which he lay with my sister; and when he spoke to her she remained silent and I made all the replies in order that he should not recognize my sister's voice. I did her a kindness, was not jealous of her, and did not expose her to shame.

And if I, a creature of flesh and blood, formed of dust and ashes, was not envious of my rival and did not expose her to shame and contempt, why shouldest thou, a King who liveth eternally and art merciful, be jealous of idolatry in which there is no reality, and exile my children and let them be slain by the sword, and their enemies have done with them as they wished!"

Forthwith the mercy of the Holy One – blessed be he – was stirred, and he said:

"For thy sake, Rachel, I will restore Israel to their place".

(*Lam R.* Prelude 24)

With refined ability the text records that alongside the 'merits' of the Fathers are also to be numbered those of the Mothers of Israel. The generous goodness of Rachel towards her sister and her courageous arguing stir the mercy of the Holy One.

The life that will eventually come forth from their womb is doubly 'grace', preceded by expectation and by prayer:

> And Isaac prayed to the Lord for his wife, because she was barren; and the Lord granted his prayer, and Rebekah his wife conceived (Gen 25:21).

On the other hand, Leah, who is unattractive and is given second place, has God's blessing on her side and gives many sons to her husband:

> When the Lord saw that Leah was hated, he opened her womb; but Rachel was barren.
> And Leah conceived and bore a son, and she called his name Reuben; for she said, "Because the Lord has looked upon my affliction; surely now my husband will love me" (Gen 29:31-32).

It seems, therefore, to the sacred author, that this situation of sterility/fertility is dependent upon the God who reveals his justice already on this earth. Rachel, beautiful and beloved, who seems thereby to have everything, in fact does not possess all, because she is sterile. Leah, less gifted by nature and for this reason less loved, however is fertile. So a certain balance is created between the two sisters and their influence on the husband.

In fact, in giving birth for the third time, Leah can say with satisfaction, "Now this time my husband will be joined to me, because I have borne him three sons!" (Gen 29:34). What Leah aspires to above all is the attention and affection of her husband. Only at the birth of the fourth son, is she confident enough of her husband's love to burst forth in uninhibited praise, "This time I will praise the Lord!" (Gen 29:35). It is the birth of Judah, the heir to the blessing.

Give me children or I will die!

> When Rachel saw that she bore Jacob no children, she envied her sister; and she said to Jacob, "Give me children, or I shall die!" (Gen 30:1).

It is a cry of deep anguish that borders on desperation. So great is the humiliation in relation to her older sister, not beautiful but fertile, and such is her desire to have descendants that Rachel cries out in the presence of Jacob, "Give me children, or I shall die"! (I will die of the agony of not having had any).

Luther comments, "I cannot remember ever having read anything like this in other stories. Rachel's desire to have chil-

13. GIVE ME CHILDREN OR I SHALL DIE (Gen 30:1)

Terracotta statuette from Cyprus (VI-V century BC; Paris, Louvre Museum).

dren is so great, that she prefers to die rather than remain sterile" (*In Genesim enarrationes*, WA 43, Weimar 1911, 655).

Jacob loves Rachel and therefore shares her pain, but in response to such a cry he answers with indignation, "Am I in the place of God, who has withheld from you the fruit of the womb?" (Gen 30:2). So Rachel, to have a son of her own, copies Sarah's trickery: she begs her husband to sleep with her slave, Bilhah, and so have a child through her. Thus Dan is born, and Rachel can exclaim, "God has judged me, and has also heard my voice and given me a son" (Gen 30:6).

But God has something far greater in store: not only a son through the medium of a surrogate mother, but the fruit of her womb, the end to her sterility:

> Then God remembered Rachel, and God hearkened to her and opened her womb. She conceived and bore a son, and said, "God has taken away my reproach" (Gen 30:22-23).

Joseph is born, and little wonder that Jacob should love him more than all his brothers. He is Rachel's son! Moreover, at this point, he can leave the country he has been living in and return home.

14. GOD HAS TAKEN AWAY MY DISHONOUR (Gen 30:23)

Wooden statuette of an Egyptian woman from approximately 1300 BC (London, British Museum).

Rachel, the wise woman

There is another side to the story of Rachel that is worthy of mention, an aspect that reveals her shrewdness and thereby belies the saying, 'beautiful, but stupid'. Rachel is beautiful and at the same time wise and intelligent.

The context is chapter 31 of Genesis. Jacob discloses his intention to depart to his wives and, having obtained their consent, plans the escape (Gen 31,17-18).

> Laban had gone to shear his sheep, and Rachel stole her father's household gods (Gen 31:19).

The most logical explanation of this act, which at first appears strange, is that Rachel should wish to be assured of the protection of the gods of her family for the journey and the new settlement in a foreign land. But the Jewish commentators and the Fathers of the Church have proposed an allegorical interpretation which makes Rachel something of a heroine. In fact, her stealing of the idols is interpreted as a profession of faith in the one, true God, the God of Jacob. This interpretation is supported by her subsequent behaviour:

> Now Rachel had taken the household gods and put them in the

camel's saddle, and sat upon them. Laban felt all about the tent, but did not find them.

And she said to her father, "Let not my lord be angry that I cannot rise before you, for the way of women is upon me." So he searched, but did not find the household gods (Gen 31:34-35).

The *Midrash Rabbah* attributes to Rachel the intention of freeing her father from his idols:

Her motive was truly noble, because she said, What! Are we going away and leaving the old man (Laban) in his error? For this reason, Scripture judges it necessary to inform us: Rachel stole the idols from her father (Gen R. 74:5).

St Ephrem the Syrian, who composed his commentary on Genesis between the years 364 and 370 AD, sees in Rachel's behaviour the utmost disdain for the idols, and states:

Rightly Jacob loved Rachel, who loved her God and despised her father's idols, not so much for having stolen them, as for treating them as things of no use, even to using them as a menstrual seat on the day they were searching for them (*ad loc.*).

In fact, if Rachel had truly stolen the idols because she trusted in their protection, how is it that she treats them now with such irreverence? Sitting on them is an expression of dominion. Even G. von Rad, a great modern exegete, holds that "a very sharp judgement is given concerning the unholiness and nothingness of this 'god'; a woman sat upon it in her uncleanness (cf Lev 15:19ff)" (*Genesis: a commentary*, London 1972, 310).

Rachel, therefore, believes in the God of Jacob and not in the idols of her father, which she treats as she would a filthy rag, and she sits upon them like a queen, a victorious heroine.

The prayer of Jacob

Now we follow Jacob on his return journey and join him at the River Jabbok – a tributary of the Jordan – while he is wondering how he can win the favour of his brother, Esau. He has already prepared his speech, sending messengers ahead with these words:

Thus says your servant Jacob, "I have sojourned with Laban, and stayed until now" (Gen 32:4).

The *Midrash Tanhuma* gives this explanation:

> I have become neither prince nor man of importance, but have remained a foreigner. Therefore you have no reason to hate me on account of the blessing imparted to me by your father when he said, Be a master over your brothers. Such a blessing in fact has not been fulfilled in me (Quoted from Rashi).

The fact remains that this foreigner who is returning home is still seized with fear and anguish at the thought of his brother Esau, and he beseeches the Lord:

> And Jacob said, "O God of my father Abraham and God of my father Isaac, O Lord who didst say to me, 'Return to your country and to your kindred, and I will do you good,' I am not worthy of the least of all the steadfast love and all the faithfulness which thou hast shown to thy servant, for with only my staff I crossed this Jordan; and now I have become two companies. Deliver me, I pray thee, from the hand of my brother, from the hand of Esau, for I fear him, lest he come and slay us all, the mothers with the children (Gen 32:9-11).

15. I AM NOT WORTHY OF YOUR GOODNESS (Gen 32:10)

Canaanite bronze statuette from Ascalon, Israel (IV century BC; Jerusalem, Museum of Israel).

Jacob declares himself to be unworthy of the goodwill and faithfulness of God. At Bethel he had requested only the barest necessities for survival in a strange land (bread and clothing) and to return safe and sound to his father's house.

The servant of Abraham travelled the same road bringing as gifts for Nahor ten camels and all kinds of precious goods, in exchange for the wife he had to choose for Isaac. Jacob, on the contrary, remembers having departed with nothing except his staff for the journey. Now he is rich and he owes it all to God. But there is one thing worrying him greatly: his brother, Esau, "Deliver me from the hand of my brother..." (Gen 32:12). And, once again, God reveals himself as Jacob's shepherd, freeing him from this fear.

But first there is an extraordinary experience. Jacob lets all his beasts, servants, wives and children cross the river until, left alone, he has to wrestle with a mysterious person. He wrestles until the first light of day, and although wounded in the sciatic nerve, he does not pause, but continues fighting, wanting to know the name of his adversary. The first to surrender is the mysterious person: "Let me go, for the day is breaking". But Jacob said, "I will not let you go, unless you bless me!" (Gen 32:26). That struggle leaves its mark on Jacob forever. In fact he leaves the Jabbok with another name: "Your name shall no more be called Jacob, but Israel, for you have striven with God and with men, and have prevailed!" (Gen 32:28).

Forever he will carry in his flesh the sign of that night, spent in a dramatic conflict with God. It will mark his unconditional surrender to the God of Abraham and of Isaac who appeared to him while he was fleeing towards Haran.

Arriving in his homeland, he fulfils his promise inviting the entire family to rise up, purify themselves and go up to Bethel:

> ...That I may make there an altar to the God who answered me in the day of my distress and has been with me wherever I have gone (Gen 35:3).

At the close of his life, in his blessing to the two sons of Joseph born in Egypt, Jacob can say, "The God who has led me all my life long to this day" (Gen 48:15). It is a special experience of a God who is the companion on an adventurous journey, ever supportive and fully involved in all the adversities of his life. God had truly been at his side, giving him more than he ever dared to ask for; and, first among all his gifts, the great love of his life, Rachel!

**Rachel,
the mother who dies
giving life**

We are nearing the end of Rachel's life. It is an event which is both dramatic and sublime: a death that generates life, a prelude to the great paschal mystery:

> Then they journeyed from Bethel; and when they were still some distance from Ephrath, Rachel travailed, and she had hard labour.
> And when she was in her hard labour, the midwife said to her, "Fear not; for now you will have another son."
> And as her soul was departing (for she died), she called his name Benoni; but his father called his name Benjamin (Gen 35: 16-18).

Such is the death of Rachel. This valiant woman who had cried out, "Give me children or I shall die", dies in the act of giving life to her second-born, son of her agony and therefore child of greatest blessing for Jacob. Rachel dies in order to give life. Hers is a fruitful death, rich in promise, a death that gives birth to Benjamin.

> So Rachel died, and she was buried on the way to Ephrath (that is, Bethlehem) (Gen 35:19).

That tomb, upon which Jacob erected a funerary stele, is a monument to life that bursts out of death. It is a monument to motherhood.

Rachel weeps for her children

Many centuries later that tomb is to inspire a dramatic utterance from the prophet Jeremiah:

A voice is heard in Ramah,
lamentation and bitter weeping.
Rachel is weeping for her children;
she refuses to be comforted for her children, because they are not
(Jer 31:15).

It is a reference to the tragedy of a nation that is deported to Babylon. From Rachel's tomb Jeremiah would hear the sobbing of a mother who had died in vain because the children she bore have been brutally snatched from her.

In his turn, Matthew, the evangelist, echoes that lament in his account of the slaughter of the innocents (Mt 2:18). It is the grief of a mother for every child that dies. Rachel, who has died to give life, seems to die a second time in the death of her son, and this time without any possible comfort.

A Jewish text interprets the tears of Jacob and of Rachel in Genesis 29:11 in the light of Jeremiah 31:15:

And he wept.... Why did he weep? He saw that she would not be buried with him. And she, too, wept and lamented, as it is written: Rachel weeps for her children, because she is a prophetess.

And so, that tomb is the sign not only of the mother who dies giving life but also of the mother who weeps for every child that dies; even to our own times.

The worth of the mothers of Israel

A couple of truly notable passages of the *Midrash Rabbah* reveal an almost unexpected consideration regarding women in the salvation history of Israel. The meeting of Jacob with the shepherds at the well before the arrival of Rachel is commented as follows:

And Jacob said unto them, My brethren, whence are ye? And they said, Of Haran are we (Gen 29:4). Rabbi Jose ben Hanina interpreted the passage in reference to the dispersion [of Israel]... *Of Haran are we* – we are fleeing from God's wrath (*haron*).

And he said unto them, Know ye Laban the son of Nahor? (Gen 29:5) – know ye him who will one day make your iniquities white (*labben*) as snow?

16. LAMENTATION AND BITTER WEEPING
(Jer 31:15)

Egyptian mourners. Parietal fresco from the tomb of Ramose at Thebes (1372-1354 BC).

39

And he said unto them, Is it well with him? And they said, It is well (Gen 29:6). For whose sake? – *And, behold, Rachel his daughter cometh with the sheep* (ibid.). Thus it is written, Thus saith the Lord, A voice is heard in Ramah, lamentation, and bitter weeping, Rachel weeping for her children; she refuseth to be comforted....

Thus saith the Lord, Refrain thy voice from weeping.... And there is hope for thy future, saith the Lord; and thy children shall return to their own border (Jer 31:15ff). (Gen R. 70:10).

This midrashic commentary reveals in the passage from Genesis, a strong theological content employing an interpretative method often used by the ancients, both Jewish and Christian, i.e. word-play. The name of 'Laban' has the same consonants as a Hebrew verb meaning 'to be white, to whiten'. Moreover, the name 'Haran' is similar to a Hebrew term meaning 'wrath'. For this reason, in the midrashic interpretation, the shepherds of Haran are seen as the symbol of Israel in exile on account of God's wrath for their sins, while Laban is presented as the one who will one day 'whiten the sins of the people.

It is interesting here to note the motive behind the Jewish interpreter's pleasure in making such subtle connections: he intends to highlight the rôle of Rachel. It is not by means of Laban, but by the merits of his daughter, that the sins of the people are to be expiated and God will lead back the exiles. Rachel, arriving with her flock, is seen in the comprehensive rôle of her life: the mother of Israel who gives birth by grace, who dies giving life and weeps for her children in exile. Side by side with the merits of the fathers of Israel, so important in the Jewish theology of all ages, there is room also for the merits of the mothers.

17. THEY CAME INTO EPYPT
(Gen 46:6)

A bedouin caravan in the desert. Egyptian parietal painting from the tomb of prince Mentuhotep, at Beni Hasan, Egypt (II millennium BC).

Another passage of the same Midrash Rabbah considers also the rôle of Leah together with that of Rachel, with a glance towards the most famous of the sons born to each. In the comment on Genesis 29:16 we read:

> Now *Laban had two daughters* – like two beams running from end to end of the world. Each produced captains, each produced kings, from each arose slayers of lions, from each arose conquerors of countries, from each arose dividers of countries. The sacrifices brought by the son of each overrode the Sabbath. The wars waged by the descendants of both overrode the Sabbath. To each was given two nights: the night of Pharaoh and the night of Sennacherib to Leah, and the night of Gideon and the night of Mordecai to Rachel (Gen R. 70:15).

When he was 147 years old, Jacob moved to Egypt to survive the famine, his main concern was to see Rachel's firstborn, the beloved son Joseph, whom he believed dead. For him, too, the moment for the final journey was approaching. **Jacob blesses the sons of Rachel**

> After this Joseph was told, "Behold, your father is ill"; so he took with him his two sons, Manasseh and Ephraim.
> And it was told to Jacob, "Your son Joseph has come to you"; then Israel summoned his strength, and sat up in bed (Gen 48:1-2).

There follows the rite of adoption of the two sons of Joseph, a rite that has the ring of a testament. Jacob, adopting as his own the two sons of Joseph, blesses them, transmitting to them his faith as if to say, "I want my God to be your God also. Well then, God for me has been a shepherd from the first day of my life until now."

The faith that Jacob passes on to his sons has grown out of that experience of the divine promise which he had the temerity to transform into a wager: If God will truly remain with me on this journey, he shall be my God. Now, looking back over the span of his life, the elderly Jacob can say with profound conviction, "God has been my shepherd from the very beginning of my existence until today, he has walked with me and freed me from all fear."

Centuries later, his sons will echo his words, and all of Israel can sing Psalm 23 with the same confidence:

> The Lord is my shepherd…
> Even though I walk through the valley of the shadow of death,
> I fear no evil; for thou art with me (Ps 23:4).

"I fear no evil": not because in the meantime I have become cunning – 147 years have taught Jacob a great deal, not because I am intelligent, and not because I have grown rich in flocks and offspring, but because "you are with me". And so, the experience of Jacob becomes a heritage for his children and the spiritual experience of Israel.

By faith Jacob...

The New Testament presents again the figure of Jacob in the Letter to the Hebrews, where the faith of the patriarchs is remembered (Heb 11:1-40). In this context the figure of Jacob is associated with the blessing of the two sons of Joseph and not with other incidents that to us would seem greater expressions of faith. It is not said, for example, by faith, Jacob wrestled with God. Instead, in presenting Jacob's faith, the Letter to the Hebrews refers back to Genesis 48:15:

> By faith Jacob, when dying, blessed each of the sons of Joseph, bowing in worship over the head of his staff (Heb 11:21).

What could be the meaning of this leaning on the head of his staff? From the Hebrew origins there is probably a misunderstanding between the words staff and bed, which are linked by assonance. However, in this image of the staff one can detect a final reference to the pastoral experience of the aged patriarch. The staff, the only thing Jacob had when he crossed the River Jordan (Gen 32:11), supports him in the last action of his life and is all-sufficing in his final journey.

The closing scene of Jacob's life thus evokes his experience of God, recalls the staff of the divine shepherd who gently leads him to the other shore, to eternal pastures: "Your staff and your crook comfort me" (Ps 23:4).

As seen also in a passage of the *Midrash*, the mercy of God in the image of the shepherd permeates the whole life of Jacob:

> And when Jacob was asked, "And how many mercies did God show towards you? – he replied, They are without number: God... has been my shepherd throughout my whole life until today (*Midrash* Ps 118:6).

The pastoral role of the fathers and mothers

We have examined the figures of Jacob and of Rachel in connection with pastoral symbolism and we have seen the blending of human and religious experience in their story. All their experiences are carefully gathered by their descendants and treasured as a precious heritage. Their life acquires a particularly symbolic value, connected with the rôle of patriarch and matriarch. Yet, what is the true significance of such a rôle, and what could it contribute to the life of the Church in our times?

Moving through the history of Jacob we have noted, first of all, the nomadic dimension which expands into that of the fugitive, the alien, who becomes a shepherd for Laban's account. It will become clear that this experience offers the deepest roots to the biblical spirituality of the shepherd. Jacob, in

---

Jacob and his sons

And Jacob called his sons and said to them, "Gather together and I will tell you the concealed secrets, the hidden ends, the giving of the rewards of the just and the punishment of the wicked, and what the happiness of Eden is."

The twelve tribes gather together and surrounded the bed of gold on which our father Jacob was lying after the end was revealed to him and that the determined end of the blessing and the consolation might be communicated to them. (...)

They hoped that he would relate to them the determined end of the redemption and the consolation. (But) when the mystery was revealed to him, it was hidden from him and when the door was open to him, it was closed from him.

Our father Jacob answered and blessed them: each according to his good works he blessed them.

After the twelve tribes of Jacob had gathered together and surrounded the bed of gold on which our father Jacob was laying, they hoped that he was to reveal to them the order of the blessings, but it was hidden from him. Our father Jacob answered and said to them, "Abraham, my father's father, from him arose the blemished Ishmael and all the sons of Keturah. And Isaac, my father, from him arose the blemished Esau, my brother. And I fear lest there should be among you one whose heart is divided against his brothers to go and worship before foreign idols".

The twelve sons of Jacob answered together and said, "Hear us, O Israel, our father; the Lord our God is one Lord". Jacob answered and said, "Blessed be his name; may the glory of his kingdom be for ever and ever."

(*Targum Neofiti* on Gen 49:1-2)

Around the bed of the old Jacob are gathered together his sons, the twelve tribes of Israel. They are waiting for the patriarch to reveal the 'order of the blessings': who will be first, who second, and who third.... But a fear occupies the mind of the old man: that among his sons there could be a hint of idolatry.

reality, experiences the divine shepherding when he is away from his tent, a stranger and a fugitive, and thereby exposed to every danger. The two places where he meets with God – Bethel and Penuel – both find him fleeing from his brother Esau and his uncle Laban, respectively.

Within the destiny of the patriarch is inscribed that of the people: his history is a type and, in a certain sense, an anticipation of the history of Israel. In fact, it is while fleeing from Egypt, in a situation of the greatest insecurity, that the people experience in a concrete way the pastoral care of Yahweh. Likewise, Rachel, the beloved wife, cares for the flocks and is explicitly referred to as shepherdess (the only woman in the Bible to receive this title). Later on, we shall see how it is through the direct descendants of Joseph, Rachel's firstborn (or rather, the tribes of North Ephraim and Manasseh), that the symbolism of God as shepherd is preserved and transmitted.

Now, on this level of tribal ties on the one hand and of symbolism on the other, the father Jacob and the mother Rachel exercise their powerful influence of guidance and spiritual direction. Their condition as shepherds is interpreted in Jewish tradition as the foundation of spiritual leadership and endows it with its characteristic style.

Jacob is the most itinerant of all the patriarchs. In his youth he is obliged to flee to Mesopotamia, and in his old age he is forced to descend into Egypt. In this long itinerary both geographic and spiritual, he could have absorbed the influence of the two rich cultures in which he lived: that of Mesopotamia to the north and of Egypt to the south. We have seen how the pastoral symbolism was used in the literature of both Mesopotamia and Egypt to express a relationship with God which was theological and profoundly human. These aspects are also present in the Bible with the addition of a more lively sense of being a people (the God of Jacob becomes the God of Israel) and with the dimension of the exodus, that is to say, with a personal involvement of God in the liberation of the people. What bearing does all this have on present day pastoral care?

First, there is the rediscovery of the unique function of father and mother as guide, or rather of a pastoral rôle of laity and of the family. The home is regarded as the first and most natural centre for evangelization and transmission of faith, not by means of abstract definitions but according to the biblical model of the father relating to his children his personal experience of God. The ancient formula of patriarchal faith 'my God', 'the God of my fathers', or of the family, encourages this dimension to be reintroduced into the family, which is after all the nucleus of the community.

The shepherd of Jacob reveals himself as a companion on

the journey. This experience points the way to parents in their formative rôle, above all in education for life and faith. One becomes a spiritual guide by walking side by side, by sharing the hardships of travelling and the unpredictable elements the journey holds in store. With God as his companion, Jacob is able to move on with his own children, generation after generation, since God is a source of inspiration for every father.

In Judaism, the fathers and mothers of the people assume a theological relevance. Rachel, the mother who gives birth by grace and dies giving life, is one of the most expressive figures of this reality. Even after her death she continues to mourn for her children who are slaughtered and in exile; by her merits God will show mercy to Israel and bring them back to their own land. So Rachel becomes the symbol of motherhood as such. In the Christian tradition, this rôle is exercised by the Church, the mother of the faithful. It is a question of a maternity that needs to be rediscovered with reference to the laity. Side by side with the traditional figures of the ordained ministers, it is desirable that fathers and mothers of families become fathers and mothers of the Church, contributing to the generation and up-bringing of believers.

In a society in which the family appears almost to disintegrate within itself, it is of primary importance to revive the biblical experience of communicating personal faith to children. At least, in a certain sense, God remains as the God of my father and of my mother. In any case, a God who is narrated and transmitted by families which have a living experience of him, is far more attractive and credible than the God of the philosophers and theologians.

18. THERE IS HOPE FOR YOUR FUTURE (Jer 31:17)

The Hebrew people in captivity. Relief from the palace of Assurbanipal II (883-859 BC) at Nimrud, Iraq (London, British Museum).

45

MOSES AND MIRIAM

The shepherd of Israel is more than a companion for the journey. He is primarily the God who liberates: he hears the moans of the oppressed, snatches them from the hand of Egypt, and fights to bring them to safety.

In this chapter, we shall explore at greater depth the idea of pastoral care as freedom from oppression, both physical and moral, and above all from idolatry and ignorance; freedom culminating in the knowledge and service of God – the fundamental goal of the exodus.

The first figure we meet is that of Moses, the human architect of the exodus. God sends him to move his people out of Egypt (Ex 3:10) and lead them to his holy mountain, the place of revelation and of the covenant. In the framework of the Old Testament, Moses is perhaps the man who, more than any other, assumes within himself the duties of the shepherd. He is the leader of the people, the great leader and 'trail-blazer', but he is also the prophet and legislator, the one who educates Israel and nurtures them on the teaching of the *Torah*.

The one who really brings Israel out of Egypt is God, the true shepherd of the exodus. But this is not realized without human collaboration. Psalm 77:21 says:

Thou didst lead thy people like a flock
by the hand of Moses and Aaron.

The psalmist links together the name of Moses and Aaron, thereby seeing the work of both brothers as strongly associated: God has led his people by the hand of both of them. This affirmation does not come as a surprise since already in the tradition of the exodus the names of Moses and Aaron are constantly found together. However, the prophet Micah surprises us with his boldness, when he adds the name of Miriam to those of the brothers:

19. THEY MADE THE ISRAEL-ITES' LIVES BITTER (Ex1:14)

A slave being led to the court of Pharaoh Horembeb (1319-1307 BC). Relief from the tomb of the sovereign at Memphis (Leida, Rijks-museum van Oudheden).

"O my people, what have I done to you?
In what have I wearied you? Answer me!
For I brought you up from the land of Egypt,
and redeemed you from the house of bondage;
and I sent before you Moses, Aaron, and Miriam (Mic 6:3-4).

The importance which the ancient Jewish sources attribute to Miriam is remarkable and it is essentially linked to the rôle of leadership she exercised in the history of the liberation of the people of Israel. Such a rôle places her beside Moses and Aaron not only as their elder sister, but also as a charismatic woman, a leader and prophetess.

Moses and Miriam in the land of Egypt

In the Acts of the Apostles, the deacon Stephen summarizes the story of Moses, subdividing the traditional 120 years of his life into three periods of 40 years each: the first is situated in Egypt, at the court of the Pharaoh; the second in the desert of Midian, with Jethro, a shepherd-priest whose daughter he marries; then the third period is spent in carrying out the task God ordered him to do on Mount Horeb: to lead the children of Israel out of Egypt in order to serve God (Ex 3:12).

The mention of these three periods of 40 years is also found in Jewish literature. The great masters of Israel, those who were the true path-finders, are made to follow the pattern of Moses, the law-giver and teacher *par excellence*, in that their lives follow the same rhythmic pattern:

He is one of those four men who died at the age of 120 years, among whom are Moses, Hillel the Ancient, Rabban Yohanan Ben Zakkai and Rabbi Akiba.

Moses lived in Egypt for 40 years, then in Midian for 40 years, and looked after Israel for 40 years.

Hillel left Babylon at 40, he was in the service of the Sages for 40 years, and looked after Israel for 40 years.

Rabban Yohanan Ben Zakkai spent 40 years in commerce, he was in the service of the Sages for 40 years, and looked after Israel for 40 years.

Rabbi Akiba studied the Torah at the age of 40, he was in the service of the Sages for 40 years, and looked after Israel for 40 years (*Sifre* Deut 34:7).

For each of these great figures the first 40 years is, we might say, private, the second is in formation with teachers, the third is in service to the people.

20. SHALL I CALL YOU A NURSE FROM THE HEBREW WOMEN? GO! (Ex 2:7-8)

Semitic women. Detail from a parietal painting at Beni Hasan, Egypt (II millennium BC).

Miriam, the sister who keeps vigil

The one who was to lead Israel through the waters of the Red Sea is himself one who is rescued from the waters, and all because of his sister. Scripture does not mention the name of the young girl who, hidden among the reeds of the River Nile, watches closely to see what might become of her baby brother lying in a papyrus basket, but Jewish tradition has never hesitated to identify her with Miriam, the prophetess of the exodus. So, from earliest memory, the figure of Miriam is inseparable from that of Moses.

This is how the Bible tells the story:

Now a man from the house of Levi went and took to wife a daughter of Levi. The woman conceived and bore a son; and when she saw that he was a goodly child, she hid him three months. And when she could hide him no longer she took for him a basket made of bulrushes, and daubed it with bitumen and pitch; and she put the child in it and placed it among the reeds at the river's brink. And his sister stood at a distance, to know what would be done to him.

Now the daughter of Pharaoh came down to bathe at the river, and her maidens walked beside the river; she saw the basket among the reeds and sent her maid to fetch it. When she opened it she saw the child; and lo, the babe was crying. She took pity on him and said, "This is one of the Hebrews' children."

Then his sister said to Pharaoh's daughter, "Shall I go and call you a nurse from the Hebrew women to nurse the child for you?" And Pharaoh's daughter said to her, "Go."

So the girl went and called the child's mother. And Pharaoh's daughter said to her, "Take this child away, and nurse him for me, and I will give you your wages."

So the woman took the child and nursed him. And the child grew, and she brought him to Pharaoh's daughter, and he became her son; and she named him Moses, for she said, "Because I drew him out of the water" (Ex 2:1-10).

The message of this first story, which borders on legend, is most eloquent. It is God who guides the events according to his plan of salvation, to the point where the waters of the Nile, threatening death, are made to bring life to that tiny child, floating in a basket made of reeds. Without a doubt, the background is mythical, yet theological as well, but the scene is rich in details that leave room for human collaboration. Here the history of salvation passes through the co-operation of three women: the mother of the baby, his sister and the daughter of the Pharaoh.

What is said of Miriam? Inasmuch as the account makes mention of her alone with regard to Moses, some traits of her personality are already in evidence.

In the first place, she is the sister who keeps watch. She remains some distance away (merahoq), in a position which allows her to see, to hear and to help. Her standing and watching to see what might have become of her little brother is full of tenderness and responsibility. Miriam is the sister who acts as a mother who is vigilant and caring.

The Book of Jubilees adds a touching account to the biblical account:

> Your mother would come by night to give you milk (to nurse you) and during the day Miriam, your sister, protected you from the birds (47:5).

And how this little woman demonstrates her initiative and powers of persuasion! Not only does she keep vigil, but as soon as she becomes aware of a favourable circumstance, she comes out of her hiding-place and with the daring of the very young engages the daughter of the Pharaoh in conversation, puts forward her proposal and succeeds in convincing her.

It matters little if the proposal sounds paradoxical. The message is clear. This child is watched over by the Lord who intervenes to change a threatening fate into one of providence and success. However, the saving intervention of the Lord is realized through the action of Miriam: by means of her vigilance, her patient waiting and her bold initiative.

Miriam keeps watch because in that basket is the little brother she loves, and for love of him, she places her own life at risk. Now, vigilance is essentially a characteristic of the shepherd who, by definition, is one who guards and takes care of (Ps 12:4).

Such is God for Israel. Such is Miriam for Moses.

Nearing the end of the 40 years...

Moses lives the first 40 years of his life in Egypt, at that time a highly civilized country. He has the good fortune of growing up in the house of the Pharaoh, in an atmosphere of comfort and refinement. He becomes a man of substance, a man of culture, "a man with power both in his speech and in his actions", as Stephen would later say in his discourse to the Sanhedrin (Acts 7:22).

> One day, when Moses had grown up, he went out to his people and looked on their burdens; and he saw an Egyptian beating

21. THEY CAME AND DREW
WATER (Ex 2:16)

*Bronze jug (XI-X century BC;
Jerusalem, Rockefeller Archaeological Museum).*

Hebrew, one of his people. He looked this way and that, and seeing no one he killed the Egyptian and hid him in the sand. When he went out the next day, behold, two Hebrews were struggling together; and he said to the man that did the wrong, "Why do you strike your fellow?"

He answered, "Who made you a prince and a judge over us? Do you mean to kill me as you killed the Egyptian?"

Then Moses was afraid, and thought, "Surely the thing is known." When Pharaoh heard of it, he sought to kill Moses. But Moses fled from Pharaoh, and stayed in the land of Midian; and he sat down by a well (Ex 2:11-15).

The re-reading of this account in Acts 7 (Stephen's discourse) is even more intense, and highlights the psychological character of the event. On the threshold of his 40 years Moses steps out of his self-centredness (so many times he had gone outdoors and failed to see), he steps out of his comfortable lifestyle (in the court of the Pharaoh) and takes note of what is happening to others. He discovers the reality of oppression and, mature and responsible as he is, he cannot remain indifferent: he takes on the cause of the Hebrew and kills the Egyptian. But then he is obliged to flee because his own desert him:

He supposed that his brethren understood that God was giving them deliverance by his hand, but they did not understand (Acts 7:25).

This sentence does not appear in the Exodus narrative. It is a clarification on the part of Luke, giving an example of how the sacred text used to be read from its human and psychological viewpoint. It helps us to sense Moses' state of mind and his bitterness when faced with the total lack of understanding on the part of his brothers. The freedom he was proposing did not seem to interest them in the least. Even amongst the oppressed, there was a lack of cohesion and solidarity. They were quite ready to denounce him for having killed one of their enemies, rather than pull together amongst themselves. Moses had to take account of this set-back, this failure, and flee.

Like his fathers before him, Moses was an alien

Moses has to flee to save his life (Ex 2:15). This fact effects him so deeply that he names his firstborn son Gershom, giving this explanation, "since I am an alien (*ger*) in a foreign land" (Ex 2:22). This experience brings to mind Jacob presenting himself to the Pharaoh saying, "A hundred and thirty are the years of my nomadic life" (Gen 47:9). The same expression is found in

Exodus 6:4 to affirm that the patriarchs dwelt as strangers in the promised land. Like his fathers before him, Moses too knows what it is to be a stranger in a foreign land.

Another point of similarity with the story of Jacob is the scene at the well:

> Now the priest of Midian had seven daughters; and they came and drew water, and filled the troughs to water their father's flock.
>
> The shepherds came and drove them away; but Moses stood up and helped them, and watered their flock.
>
> When they came to their father Reuel, he said, "How is it that you have come so soon today?"
>
> They said, "An Egyptian delivered us out of the hand of the shepherds, and even drew water for us and watered the flock." He said to his daughters, "And where is he? Why have you left the man? Call him, that he may eat bread."
>
> And Moses was content to dwell with the man, and he gave Moses his daughter Zipporah. She bore a son, and he called his name Gershom; for he said, "I have been a sojourner in a foreign land" (Ex 2:16-22).

Like Rachel, Zipporah and her sisters are also shepherdesses. And Moses, like Jacob, demonstrates his strength and generosity by driving away the shepherds who were molesting them, and by giving water to their flock.

Thus the story of Moses follows, in various aspects, that of Jacob: he, too, has to flee; he meets the woman of his destiny at the well, and finally he becomes a shepherd like his ancestors before him, and his brothers until the Egyptians forced them to make bricks and till the fields (Ex 1:14).

To till the soil is not in itself the work of slaves, but it becomes so when imposed by force; it expresses, for all to see, the end of the friendly co-existence spoken of in Genesis 48. After giving the sons of Jacob the fertile land of Goshen for their flocks, Egypt becomes a hostile and oppressive country. Because of this transformation, Moses is able to recapture in his life as a shepherd the sociological origins of his people and of his fathers before him.

Consequently, the second forty-year span of his life unfolds in direct contrast to that preceding it. Moses accepts his entrance into the family of Reuel (elsewhere referred to as Jethro: Ex 3:1; 4:18; and 18:1); to all appearances, he sets aside his dreams of national liberation, and settles for the daily tasks of a shepherd in the service of his father-in-law. Humanly speaking it is a lean survival resulting from defeat, a painful degradation. But in reality it is not so. Moses has the fortune to live alongside a man of God, a priest, and in such an environment his personality matures especially on the religious and spiritual levels.

**Vocation and
mission of Moses**

Towards the end of his second span of 40 years, Moses arrives at the mountain of God:

> Now Moses was keeping the flock of his father-in-law, Jethro, the priest of Midian; and he led his flock to the west side of the wilderness, and came to Horeb, the mountain of God.
> And the angel of the Lord appeared to him in a flame of fire out of the midst of a bush; and he looked, and lo, the bush was burning, yet it was not consumed.
> And Moses said, "I will turn aside and see this great sight, why the bush is not burnt."
> When the Lord saw that he turned aside to see, God called to him out of the bush, "Moses, Moses!" And he said, "Here I am."
> Then he said, "Do not come near; put off your shoes from your feet, for the place on which you are standing is holy ground."
> And he said, "I am the God of your father, the God of Abraham, the God of Isaac, and the God of Jacob." And Moses hid his face, for he was afraid to look at God (Ex 3:1-6).

Here we are confronted with a fundamental episode in the salvation history of Israel. The mighty spectacle of the flaming bush that does not burn is an irresistible attraction for our shepherd. From within that bush, he hears himself called twice, as was Abraham (Gen 22:1): "Moses, Moses!" His reply is immediate (as was Abraham's): "Here I am".

The account highlights both the transcendence and holiness of God: Moses is treading on holy ground, and so is told to remove his sandals and adore. Yet, the Holy One who is speaking to him is not distant and unknown. He is the God of his father, who will be for him what he had been for Abraham, Isaac and Jacob: a companion on the journey.

Translating Exodus 3:5, the *Jerusalem Targum* presents an interesting amplification with allusion to the magisterial rôle of Moses. The place where he is pasturing the sheep of Jethro is the very place where he will one day receive the Law to impart to the people:

> The Lord said to Moses, "Do not come near! Take off your sandals because the place where you are standing is holy ground, and it is there that you are destined to receive the Law, in order to teach it to the children of Israel".

22. TAKE OFF YOUR
SANDALS (Ex 3:5)

Egyptian leather sandals (III millennium BC; Turin, Egyptian Museum).

In the theophany at Horeb, God reveals himself to Moses as the true protagonist of the exodus, the devisor of a liberation which is to be totally gracious. It is he who made the first move to descend for the liberation of his people (exodus from above to below). Beginning from Exodus 3:7, the verbs are all in the first person and underline the total involvement of Yahweh: 'I have seen precisely', 'I have heard', 'I know', 'I have come down', etc.

God comes down to liberate the Hebrews not because they have raised prayers and supplications (words totally absent in the sacred text), but rather because of their moans and cries of anguish typical of any people under oppression. And the moans of the oppressed are irresistible for the God of Jacob. In Exodus 2:23 we read: "The Israelites groaned because of their slavery, raising cries of lament, and their cries ascended to God". This aspect of divine grace is even more explicit in Exodus 3:7-10.

> Then the Lord said, "I have seen the affliction of my people who are in Egypt, and have heard their cry because of their taskmasters; I know their sufferings, and I have come down to deliver them out of the hand of the Egyptians, and to bring them up out of that land to a good and broad land, a land flowing with milk and honey, to the place of the Canaanites, the Hittites, the Amorites, the Perizzites, the Hivites, and the Jebusites. And now, behold, the cry of the people of Israel has come to me, and I have seen the oppression with which the Egyptians oppress them. Come, I will send you to Pharaoh that you may bring forth my people, the sons of Israel, out of Egypt."

Moses is about 80 years old when God sends him back to Egypt to do in his name what he had desired to do 40 years earlier in his own right. The God of his fathers is a God who knows of the suffering of his people and takes a stand in their defence. He wants to do this through him, but Moses voices his reservations:

> Who am I that I should go to Pharaoh, and bring the sons of Israel out of Egypt? (Ex 3:11)

But God reassures him and gives him a sign:

> I will be with you; and this shall be the sign for you, that I have sent you: when you have brought forth the people out of Egypt, you shall serve God upon this mountain (Ex 3:12).

Note the connection between the beginning and the conclusion of this passage:

3:1   Moses came to the *mountain of God*

3:12   when you have brought forth the people out of Egypt, you shall serve God upon *this mountain*.

This literary connection carries a message: after meeting the God of his fathers, Moses is sent to bring the people out and lead them to the mountain, there to serve God or rather, to adore and render homage. The *Targum* of Exodus 3:12, amplifying the biblical text, recalling that on that same mountain Israel receives the Law:

> God said: My Word will assist you. And this will be the sign for you that it is I who sent you: when you have led the people out of Egypt, you will pay homage before Yahweh, because you will receive the Law on this mountain (*Targum* Add. 27301).

Moses is, therefore, sent back in order to bring the people to the place where he has already arrived. Because of his experience he is now able to lead them to the mountain of God; as an alpine guide, whom one trusts not because he has studied the terrain on a map, but because, having himself climbed to the summit, he can lead others in safety by the route he actually knows.

This dimension of personal experience, this knowing not by hearsay, but by practical and personal effort, has always been appreciated in the Judaic tradition, as is evident in some charming anecdotes. The humaneness and tenderness of Moses ("more humble than any man on the face of the earth", Num 12:3) do not appear suddenly when he leads Israel out of Egypt; they come from long ago and affirm the importance of daily living.

The teachers of Israel relate that God calls him to take responsibility for his people because he has been meek and gentle with the sheep of Jethro:

> When Moses our teacher, peace be upon him, was tending the flock of Jethro in the wilderness, a little kid escaped from him. He ran after it until it reached a shady place. When it reached the shady place, there appeared to view a pool of water and the kid stopped to drink. When Moses approached it, he said, "I did not know that you ran away because of thirst; you must be weary". So he placed the kid on his shoulder and walked away. Thereupon God said, "Because thou hast mercy in leading the flock of a mortal, thou wilt assuredly tend my flock Israel" (Ex R. 2:2).

In the same context, the *Midrash* presents a characteristic of God's behaviour towards the leaders of Israel:

> Before God confers greatness on a man he first tests him by a little thing and then promotes him to greatness. Here you have two great leaders whom God first proved by a little thing, found trustworthy, and then promoted to greatness. He tested David with

sheep which he led through the wilderness, only in order to keep them from robbing [private fields] (...).

Similarly in the case of Moses it says: *And he led the flock to the farthest end of the wilderness* – in order to keep them from despoiling [the fields of others]. God took him to tend Israel, as it is said: *Thou didst lead thy people like a flock, by the hand of Moses and of Aaron*, Ps 77:21 (Ex R. 2:3).

Even the *Samaritan Targum* (*Memar Marqah*) connects the mission given by God to Moses with the task of the shepherd and interprets it as a teaching of the Torah. For this reason, Moses is proclaimed as the 'source of light' for the entire human family:

O great prophet Moses, fount of light for the entire family of the human race, leave the things which occupy you at present. You are not like you used to be. "Remove the sandals from your feet" (Ex 3:5) because today you must tread a holy path. Restore to their owner the sheep you are caring for, because you are at the point of governing the stars of Abraham (*Memar Marqah*, I §2).

The staff of Moses

In Exodus 4:2 we find a detail concerning the rod (*matteh*), clearly pointing to pastoral symbolism:

Then Moses answered, "But behold, they will not believe me or listen to my voice, for they will say, 'The Lord did not appear to you.'"
The Lord said to him, "What is that in your hand?"
He said, "A rod." (Ex 4:1-2).

Numerous things have been written about this rod which will change into a serpent and later be the instrument of many miracles (Ex 7:20; 9:23; 10:13). In it could be contained many symbolic elements, which partly escape us, but that must have been notable in that environment (even the sorcerers of Egypt are able to transform a rod into a serpent, Ex 7:9-11).

The rod of Moses is a sign of the authority that comes from God, explicitly stated in Exodus 4:17: "And you shall take in your hand this rod, with which you shall do the signs". Therefore, from Exodus 4:20 onwards, it becomes known as 'the rod of God'.

Yet, Moses had already had that rod in hand (Ex 4:2) and it was the instrument of his labour (Ex 3:2). In other words, the shepherd's rod is now a symbol of his authority over Israel. Moses takes it with him when he departs from Midian.

23. WHAT IS THAT IN YOUR HAND? A ROD (Ex 4:2)

Fragment from an anthropomorphic sarcophagus coming from Beirut, Lebanon (V-IV century BC; Istanbul, Archaeological Museum).

So Moses took his wife and his sons and set them on an ass, and went back to the land of Egypt; and in his hand Moses took the rod of God (Ex 4:20).

With it he will open up the sea and let the flock of the Lord pass through on dry ground (Ex 14:16). In contrast to Joshua (Josh 8:1-26), he makes use of a rod, not a weapon, to open the way towards freedom.

The prophetess Miriam

In this context we meet also the work of Miriam, whose name recalls the bondage in Egypt. In the Canticle of the Midrash we read that: "Her name is Miriam because Miriam comes from *merur* (bitterness)" (Ct R. 2,11); and in the *Midrash* of the Exodus is the confirmation: "God sent a redeemer (*go'el*), to the people, that is to say Miriam, whose name comes from *merur*" (Ex R. 26:1).

Miriam, therefore, by her very name, is a reminder of the bitterness of slavery and at the same time of the mighty intervention of he who transformed the bitterness into song. Thus in Miriam, God sent his people a *go'el*, a saviour.

The rod of Moses

Rabbi Levi said, "That rod which was created in the twilight was delivered to the first man out of the garden of Eden. Adam delivered it to Enoch, and Enoch delivered it to Noah, and Noah [handed it on] to Shem. Shem passed it on to Abraham, Abraham [transmitted it] to Isaac, and Isaac (gave it over) to Jacob, and Jacob brought it down into Egypt and passed it on to his son Joseph, and when Joseph died and they pillaged his household goods, it was placed in the palace of Pharaoh. And Jethro was one of the magicians of Egypt, and he saw the rod and the letters which were upon it, and he desired in his heart (to have it), and he took it and brought it, and planted it in the midst of the garden of his house. No one was able to approach it any more.

When Moses came to his house he went into the garden of Jethro's house, and saw the rod and read the letters which were upon it, and he put forth his hand and took it. Jethro watched Moses, and said: This one in the future will redeem Israel from Egypt. Therefore he gave him Zipporah his daughter to wife, as it is said, *And Moses was content to dwell with the man; and he gave Moses Zipporah, his daughter* (Ex 2:21).

(Pirke of Rabbi Eliezer, ch. 40)

The miraculous rod of Moses is surrounded, in the Jewish tradition, with an aura of legend that has attempted to identify the source of its mysterious power. Created in the twilight of the first Sabbath, the rod came to have inscribed on it the letters which depict the Name of God.

The *Babylonian Talmud* numbers her among the seven prophetesses of Israel: Sarah, Miriam, Deborah, Hannah, Abigail, Hulda and Esther. It is not an unmerited title since Scripture itself named her 'prophetess' in Exodus 15:20.

According to the Judaic tradition, Miriam prophesied the birth of Moses and the singular task the Lord was to entrust to the child: to deliver Israel from slavery. But her prophecy seemed to be discredited since it appeared to remain only half-fulfilled. In actual fact, the joy at the birth of the child was immediately shattered by the sentence of death that applied to every new-born male Hebrew.

It was not easy to see how God could save his people by means of a baby thrown into the waters of the Nile! Miriam, however, does not concede defeat, she waits to see. Her expectation receives its first reply when Moses is received and saved by the daughter of the Pharaoh, but it is only in Exodus 15:20 that her hope is completely fulfilled when she sees her brother and all the people rising out of the sea. Then, Moses is no longer the one who was saved, but he becomes a saviour as Miriam had prophesied.

This is how the rabbinic interpretation reads the Bible with the Bible, in our case Exodus 2:4 with Exodus 15:20.

The woman who leads the dance

Moses and Miriam appear together on the shores of the Red Sea. Both sing and lead the people in song in honour of Yahweh. It is the famous text known as 'The song of the sea', one of the most ancient passages in Scripture:

The prophecy of Miriam

Was she only the sister of Aaron and not the sister of Moses? — Rabbi Nahman said in the name of Rab: [She was so called] because she prophesied when she was the sister of Aaron [only] and said, My mother is destined to bear a son who will save Israel. When he was born the whole house was filled with light, and her father arose and kissed her on the head, say-ing, My daughter, thy prophecy has been fulfilled. But when they threw him into the river her father arose and tapped her on the head, say-ing, Daughter, where is thy prophecy? So it is written, And his sister stood afar off to know; to know, [that is,] what would be with the latter part of her prophecy.

(*Babylonian Talmud,* Megillah 14a)

In Exodus 15:20 Miriam is presented as 'sister of Aaron'. On this curious fact a disciple questions his rabbi.

> Then Miriam, the prophetess, the sister of Aaron, took a timbrel in her hand; and all the women went out after her with timbrels and dancing (Ex 15:20).

It is Miriam who teaches and intones the song, from the moment that she formulates the theme in the chorus, to be repeated by the entire assembly:

> And Miriam sang to them, "Sing to the Lord for he has triumphed gloriously; the horse and his rider he has thrown into the sea" (Ex 15:21).

This woman who sings and dances with so much enthusiasm and appears to be in the full vigour of her youth must in fact be about 90 years old, going by the indication found in Exodus 7:7. All the more reason then to admire her, since her enthusiasm, at her great age, is so contagious that it draws all the women of Israel to sing and dance in honour of the victory of Yahweh over the Pharaoh and his warriors.

Perhaps every Hebrew mother has taught her son that song of a victory beyond all expectation and of an escape from danger to freedom at least once in her lifetime. The long procession of women initiated by Miriam continues through time and across many generations.

It is significant that the *Targum* repeats the scene of Exodus 15 also in Psalm 68: "The singers in front, the musicians last, between them the maidens playing tambourines" (v. 26). The commentary states:

> They hurried and uttered the song, following Moses and Aaron who were singing before them, in the midst the just women who were playing the tambourines with Miriam (*Targum* Ps 68:26).

Here the singing and dancing of the women do not celebrate the prowess of the husbands and brother warriors, as for example in 1 Samuel 18:6-7:

> As they were coming home, when David returned from slaying the Philistine, the women came out of all the cities of Israel, singing and dancing, to meet King Saul, with timbrels, with songs of joy, and with instruments of music.
>
> And the women sang to one another as they made merry, "Saul has slain his thousands, and David his ten thousands."

On the shores of the Red Sea – the Sea of Reeds, as the Bible calls it – the daughters of Israel, headed by Miriam, interweave dances with chorus and song to celebrate the work of the Lord.

It is not warriors who have won, nor the men of Moses and Aaron; the Lord alone has triumphed wonderfully.

Miriam, the prophetess, addresses her sentiments of exultation to the real protagonist; she prevents the feast from degenerating into self-complacency and sings for Yahweh, the only mighty and victorious one. Her song directs the praise to the Lord, who alone is majestic in holiness and worker of wonders. This is how the *Targum* amplifies Miriam's refrain:

> We glorify and sing praises before the Lord, because power and grandeur belong to him: above all the proud he is exalted and above all the great he is elevated. Because the ungodly Pharaoh rebelled against Yahweh and pursued the people of the sons of Israel, Yahweh has thrown his horses and chariots into the Sea of Reeds and submerged them (*Targum* Add. 27301).

25. THE HORSE AND HIS RIDER HE HAS THROWN INTO THE SEA (Ex 15:1)

The Pharaoh Tutankamen (1333-1323 BC) on his war chariot. Painting on a side of his wooden sarcophagus discovered at Thebes (Cairo, Egyptian Museum).

The 40 years in the desert

The fall of the enemy finds expression in song, but it is not enough to forge the new life of liberty. The crossing the Red Sea does not result immediately in the ability to enjoy freedom. This requires time and a patient apprenticeship. For Israel, the 40 years' wandering in the desert is a novitiate of freedom. Confronted with the lack of bread and water, the people have to learn the freedom of children who trust in God. In the silence of the desert (*midbar*), Israel will be schooled in receiving the word (*dabar*) of the law of freedom, to have access to the sanctuary (*debir*), the tent of intimacy with God.

It is certainly not by chance that the first sanctuary of Israel, built under God's instruction to Moses, is a tent, that is the dwelling of nomadic shepherds. Yahweh, too, was a nomad in those years, journeying beside his people, under the tent.

In the wanderings of the desert, God in the first place, and then Moses and also Miriam, show themselves to be good shepherds for Israel, assuring them of protection and vigilance, and never allowing them to lack what was necessary.

The people feared they would die of thirst, having walked for three days without finding water. When at last they find it, it is not drinkable: it is bitter. So they murmur against Moses, "What shall we drink? (Ex 15:24). Why did you lead us out of Egypt to let us die of thirst, us and our children and our flock?" (Ex 17:3).

The chorus of laments is not exhausted with the miracle of the water. It reappears punctually when the food runs out:

> Would that we had died by the hand of the Lord in the land of Egypt, when we sat by the fleshpots and ate bread to the full; for you have brought us out into this wilderness to kill this whole assembly with hunger (Ex 16:3).

The anguish of death, expressed in the murmuring against Moses, becomes nostalgia for the past, the times in which even with hardship it was possible to survive. Now the glorious time of liberation is cursed because it marks the beginning of adversities, the opening towards death.

In Psalm 78, which in the form of a recitation meditates on the history of Israel, the memory is focussed on that murmuring with a crucial question: "Can God spread a table in the wilderness?" (Ps 78:19). Well, yes, God did spread a table for Israel in the wilderness. And he proved himself as a good shepherd in leading his people in the desert for 40 years without their ever having lacked anything. A Judaic tradition recounts:

> Just as sheep do not have stores [of fodder] prepared for them, but graze on what they can find every day, so Israel had no provision stored up for them, save [that which they found] in the wilderness, as it says, *And the people shall go out and gather a day's portion every day,* Ex 16:4 (Ex R. 24:3).

Israel expected to die of hunger. Instead, they gathered a bread that they had not laboured to sow, and they ate every day, without needing to accumulate – "sheep do not have stores prepared for them". The manna had to be gathered daily, as much as sufficed, "according to the number of the persons whom each of you has in his tent " (Ex 16:16).

So Israel learned to trust in God, day by day, gathering the daily bread. The expression in Psalm 78: "Can God spread a table (*la 'arok shulhan*) in the wilderness?" recurs, no longer as a provocative question, but rather as an observation full of gratitude in Psalm 23, known as the psalm of the good shepherd, "You prepare a table for me (*ta 'arok... shulhan*) in the presence of my enemies" (Ps 23:5).

In following the shepherd Yahweh, Israel lacks nothing practically. The table prepared indicates the providence experienced throughout all those years, and so, too, the word of the Law which substantially nurtured the people at the foot of Mount Sinai. This connection is well evidenced in Deuteronomy in the context of the second discourse of Moses:

> And you shall remember all the way which the Lord your God has led you these 40 years in the wilderness, that he might humble you, testing you to know what was in your heart, whether you would keep his commandments, or not.
> And he humbled you and let you hunger and fed you with manna, which you did not know, nor did your fathers know; that he might make you know that man does not live by bread alone, but that man lives by everything that proceeds out of the mouth of the Lord.
> Your clothing did not wear out upon you, and your foot did not swell, these 40 years (Deut 8:2-4).

Rabbi Yehudah calls to mind that the journey implies three things: it wears out the clothing of man, it reduces his bodily weight and diminishes his supply of money. But this is not verified in the case of Israel during 40 years spent in the desert, inasmuch as "the last day in the desert for the children of Israel was like the first" (*Midrash* on Psalms).

Other rabbinical explanations connect the pastoral care of Yahweh with vigilance and protection:

> As a shepherd keeps watch over his flock against wolves day and night, so the Holy One, blessed be he, kept watch over Israel, since it is written: "The pillar of cloud did not depart by day" (Ex 13:22). So also in the future: "A tent will make a shadow by day" (Is 4:6). It is written: "You have led your people like a flock by the hand of Moses and Aaron", Ps 77:21 (*Yalqut Shim'oni* II, 843b).
> Just as sheep do not enter under the shadow of a roof, so also did God lead Israel 40 years in the wilderness (Ex R. 24:3).

In the last analysis, the 40 years' wandering in the desert constituted the school of experience where Israel learned to trust in God, not in an intentional manner, but through countless

26. HE LET YOU HUNGER AND THEN FED YOU (Deut 8:3)

A man at prayer. Detail from a parietal relief from the palace of Sennacherib (704-681 BC) at Nineveh, Iraq (London, British Museum).

affirmations of affection, experiencing concretely the care and providence of Yahweh, whether directly, or through the mediation of Moses and Miriam.

The tent in the desert

The nomadic-pastoral dimension experienced by Israel in the 40 years in the desert is well illustrated by the tent. To this day, it remains the main characteristic of the feast of *Sukkot*, or shelters, which recalls the years of nomadic living when the Lord led Israel out of Egypt (cf Lev 23:23-36, 39-43).

The tent, as the house, speaks of protection and intimacy, but, unlike the house, it is a dwelling suited to travelling. A dwelling that marks the stages of the journey: "Then Moses led Israel onward from the Red Sea..." (Ex 15:22). At each stopping-place, the tent is erected to enable the family group to gather together in unity for the sharing of food and for rest.

Significantly, the sanctuary Moses ordered to be constructed had the shape of a tent and occupied a central position in the camp. The Book of Exodus dedicates a great deal of space to the matter. Seven chapters (Ex 25-31) deal with the prescriptions received by Moses on the mountain with reference to the construction of the sanctuary, the furnishings and the ministers who were to conduct the worship; and six more chapters (Ex 35-40) relate the performance of tasks, including the erection and consecration of the sanctuary. Actually, it is with God's act of taking possession of the holy place that the Book of Exodus concludes, thus adding to the importance of this subject and its symbolism.

The concluding image is of the people of God on the journey, led by the tent of Yahweh (the tabernacle):

> Throughout all their journeys, whenever the cloud was taken up from over the tabernacle, the people of Israel would go onward; but if the cloud was not taken up, then they did not go onward till the day that it was taken up. For throughout all their journeys the cloud of the Lord was upon the tabernacle by day, and fire was in it by night, in the sight of all the house of Israel (Ex 40:36-38).

27. THE ARK OF THE LORD WENT BEFORE THEM (Num 10:33)

Ark carried in procession by four priests. Detail from the temple of Amon at Karnak (XIV-XIII century BC; Leida, Rijks-museum van Oud-heden).

This image of the tent, the dwelling-place of God who walks with his people, is rich in symbolic memories. Besides the itinerant movement, to which the folding-the-tent alludes (to indicate stages of the journey in the desert), a prominent aspect is found in the symbolism of welcome and hospitality. To enter the tent is to receive the generous hospitality of the nomad and protection (cf Gen 18:1-5). The symbolism is present in various texts which speak of the temple of Jerusalem using the ancient image of the tent, as for example in Psalm 15:1: "O Lord, who shall sojourn in thy tent? Who shall dwell on thy holy hill?".

The tent of Moses

Yet the tent is also associated with the theme of instruction. To this end there is a significant episode in Exodus 18, where we read of the visit of Jethro, the priest of Midian who received the fugitive Moses into his tent, inviting him to eat at his table and thereby to enter fully into the intimacy of his family life. Hearing "of all that God had done for Moses and for Israel" (Ex 18:1), Jethro decided to pay a visit to his son-in-law. The meeting is described vividly and highlights the symbolism of the tent: "Moses went out to meet his father-in-law, and did obeisance and kissed him; and they asked each other of their welfare, and went into the tent" (Ex 18:7).

The narrative reveals how under that tent the two men of God were mutually enlightened. "Moses told his father-in-law all that the Lord had done to Pharaoh and to the Egyptians for Israel's sake" (Ex 18:8). His account was both a doxology and a catechesis, for Moses gave glory to the Lord and at the same time enlightened his father-in-law regarding the greatness of Yahweh.

In his turn, Jethro "rejoiced for all the good which the Lord had done to Israel". His words are evidence, if not exactly of a conversion, at least of an explicit acknowledgment of the supremacy of Yahweh:

> "Blessed be the Lord, who has delivered you out of the hand of the Egyptians and out of the hand of Pharaoh. Now I know that the Lord is greater than all gods, because he delivered the people from under the hand of the Egyptians, when they dealt arrogantly with them" (Ex 18:10-11).

The tent of Moses is, therefore, a place of welcome and of exchange: at the human and spiritual level. It is a place where even one who does not belong to the people of Israel can hear of the wonders performed by the Lord and join in blessing him!

The rest of the account narrates that the following day, "Moses took his seat to administer justice for the people" (Ex 18:13). We do not know from the text exactly where this took place, but it is highly probable that it was near the borders of his tent. For, it was there that Abraham was sitting when he saw the three men who were coming to visit him (Gen 18:1). Jethro was still present and he was overwhelmed by the volume of work weighing upon his son-in-law:

"What is this that you are doing for the people? Why do you sit alone, and all the people stand about you from morning till evening?" And Moses said to his father-in-law, "Because the people come to me to inquire of God; when they have a dispute, they come to me and I decide between a man and his neighbour, and I make them know the statutes of God and his decisions" (Ex 18:14-16).

Thus the tent, in this second part of the narrative, is the place where Moses sits in judgement, to render justice to the people and to teach them the will of God – his laws and his decrees.

Within his tent Moses receives anyone who has need of his help; there he listens to them, he teaches and imparts justice. In other words, he forms consciences and educates a people.

We shall see later how the Judaic interpretation developed the relationship between tent and teaching, even to the point of equating the shepherds' tents, with the houses used for teaching the *Torah*.

The tent of Yahweh

If the tent of Moses evokes such a rich experience, what can be said of the tent of Yahweh, where the Lord himself has descended and taken up his abode (Ex 40:34-35)?

According to the *Midrash* of Exodus 25:2, the tent of Yahweh is erected because he is unable to separate himself from the *Torah* he has given to his people. He is like a king who gave his only daughter to a young man, but then begged him to prepare a room for him, so that he could go and see his daughter whenever he desired.

Another comment unites Law and tent in the sign of the bridal love of God for his people, making use of Deuteronomy 33:4 to comment on Exodus 25:1:

> "Moses commanded us a law, as a possession (*morashah*) for the assembly of Jacob..." – Do not read the word as *morashah* but *me'orasah* (betrothed), for just as a bridegroom, so long as he has not married his betrothed, is a visitor at the house of his father-in-law; after he has married her, her father comes to her. Thus before the *Torah* was given to Israel, '*Moses went up unto God*' (Ex 19:3), but after the Torah had been given, God said to Moses: "And let them make me a sanctuary, that I may dwell among them", Ex 25:8 (Ex R. 33:7).

More so than any other, the tent of Yahweh is the place of hospitality and meeting. But here, the host and the guests are two extremely different realities: God and humanity, the creator and creature. Entering the tent of the Lord therefore, signifies primarily, humanity's discovery of mercy and salvation. Consequently, the experience of being welcomed and forgiven causes songs of praise and thanks to burst forth.

In this sense, the tent of Yahweh is the place of worship and of prayer. The Judaic tradition specifically highlights Moses' prayer of intercession. With amazing audacity, born of love for his people and the conviction that they belong to God, Moses addresses himself to the Lord in these words:

> Moses said to the presence of the Place (God), "Lord of all times, you did not make Israel leave Egypt in order to punish them if they sin, but in order, if they sin, to pardon them. You did not make Israel leave Egypt in order that they not have guides, but in order that they may have guides" (*Yalqut Shim'oni* I, 843b).

In Judaic tradition, Moses is presented as one who is truly capable of being a leader, a shepherd who watches over his flock and feels responsible for his sheep. The *Midrash Rabbah* comments on Exodus 15:22 ("Moses then led Israel from the

The pastoral rôles of Moses and Miriam

The king, the daughter and the tent

Can you conceive a transaction in which the seller is sold his own goods! God, however, said to Israel, "I have sold you my *Torah*, but with it, as it were, I also have been sold", as it says, "*that they take me for an offering*" (Ex 25:2).

It can be compared to the only daughter of a king whom another king married. When he wished to return to his country and take his wife with him, he [the father] said to him, "My daughter, whose hand I have given thee, is my only child. I cannot part with her, neither can I say to thee, 'Do not take her', for she is now thy wife. This favour, however, I would request of thee; wherever thou goest to live, have a chamber ready for me that I may dwell with you, for I cannot leave my daughter."

Thus God said to Israel, "I have given you a *Torah* from which I cannot part, and I also cannot tell you not to take it; but this I would request: wherever you go make for me a house wherein I may sojourn", as it says, "And let them make me a sanctuary, that I may dwell in their midst" (Ex 25:8).

(Ex R. 33:1)

The Midrash *does not hesitate to force the original text of Ex 25:2 – it reads: "tell them to take me for an offering" instead of: "tell them to take an offering for me!" – in order to draw out the connection that God has willed between the tent (the sanctuary in the desert, model of the future temple), the law and Israel. The link is the love of the Father.*

Red Sea") in the sense of a perfect understanding and reciprocity between leaders and people. Moses had succeeded in gaining for himself the confidence of Israel:

> Just as sheep follow the shepherd whithersoever they are led, so did Israel also follow Moses whithersoever he led them, as it says, "Draw me, we will run after thee", Ct 1:4 (Ex R. 24:3).

But why was Moses likened to a good shepherd? – asks a disciple of the rabbi. Because – he explains in a beautiful interpretation of Ezekiel 13:5 – unlike the false prophets who cared only for their personal interests, Moses kept watch over Israel, 'he remained standing' in the moment of need and of danger:

> You have not gone up into the breaches (Ezek 13:5) like Moses. And why did Moses act like a good shepherd? Because if the flock's enclosure collapsed on the evening of the sabbath, in the darkness he stayed on his feet and repaired it; and if there remained a breach, he stayed there on his feet; if a lion came, he stayed on his feet against it (*Yalqut Shim'oni*, II 837b).

To this same question another rabbi offered the following reply:

> Because when the owner of his flock (God) said to him, "Leave my flock!", he replied "I will not leave until you make known to me who you will appoint in my place!" (The order follows, from God, to anoint Joshua as his successor – *Midrash Haggadol* on Num 27:17).

This interpretation throws light on Moses' social responsibility. The great legislator and educator of the people concerns himself with providing continuity to his work. He finds a successor so that Israel will not become disorientated without any help or control, like a flock without a shepherd. In fact, in Numbers 27:12, it is written that the Lord warned Moses of his imminent death, and Moses said to him:

> "Let the Lord, the God of the spirits of all flesh, appoint a man over the congregation, who shall go out before them and come in before them, who shall lead them out and bring them in; that the congregation of the Lord may not be as sheep which have no shepherd" (Num 27:16-17).

According to the *Aboth* of Rabbi Nathan, the Lord gave this reply to Moses:

Thereupon the Holy One, blessed be he, said to Moses, "Go and appoint for him an interpreter that he may expound (the *Torah*) in your presence at the head of the notables of Israel".

At that time Moses said to Joshua, "Joshua, as for this people that I am delivering into your charge, they are not he-goats but kids; I am not delivering to you sheep but lambs, because as yet they have not occupied themselves with the commandments, and so have not reached the stage of he-goats; as it is stated, *If thou know not, O thou fairest among women, go thy way forth by the footsteps of the flock and feed thy kids beside the shepherds' tents* , Ct 1: 8 (*Abot* de Rabbi Natan 17:3).

Moses, therefore, wants Joshua to shepherd with gentleness the people of Israel, when he explains to them the *Torah*. They are not comparable, in fact, to goats and sheep, since they still resemble tender kids and lambs inasmuch as they have not been instructed in the commandments. To this end, he procures for them an *amorà* (teacher, interpreter), namely, an expert who assists him and communicates his doctrine in a way acceptable to the people.

On the basis of this interpretation, we can see the link between shepherd and teacher, a link which we will study further in the following chapters. The rôle of Joshua as 'shepherd' is explained primarily by his instructing the people in the *Torah*, just as the good shepherd Moses had done.

So it is no coincidence that Miriam, too, is recognized as fulfilling the rôle of leader and guide in the departure from Egypt, alongside Moses and Aaron. The most explicit recognition of this is to be found in Micah 6:4, where her function as leader is singled out amongst the great works of the Lord.

Miriam is a woman who precedes, who 'walks ahead', language which designates the rôle of the shepherd who walks in front of his flock. Moreover, in the Judaic tradition, she is attributed with a pastoral rôle.

Moses, Aaron and Miriam are held to be the three faithful shepherds of the Exodus, pre-announced by Joseph when he interpreted the dream (for the cup-bearer of the Pharaoh) of the vine with the three branches (Gen 40:9-11). The *Targum* of Micah 6:4 clarifies the limits of their respective authority:

I sent before you three prophets: Moses to teach the tradition on judgements (cf Ex 18), Aaron to perform the rite of expiation over the people (Num 17) and Miriam to instruct the women (Ex 15:20-21) (Le Deaut, *Miriam*, 214).

In brief, the prophetic-pastoral rôle of Miriam unfolds in terms of teaching the Torah – she is the pioneer of women rabbis and theologians! – and in animating the liturgy. It could be said that Miriam demonstrates how the two can be integrated. Her prophecy finds expression in music and song. In other words, the most sublime teaching is that which reaches the heart and results in praise.

With her lively prophecy, full of charisma and poetic inspiration, Miriam carried out effectively her rôle as spiritual leader among the daughters and sons of Israel. And her influence is alive even today.

Without Miriam we cannot move on

We find the figure of Miriam again in Numbers 12, a narrative that at first glance does not honour her. She is aligned with Aaron against Moses, their brother, whom they accuse of having married an alien woman; but behind this criticism is probably concealed a sense of jealousy. On account of this, she is stricken with leprosy.

She also has to suffer the consequences of the sin of Aaron on his behalf, he being spared the humiliating punishment on account of his priestly dignity (the leper is considered impure, Lev 22:4). Aaron pleads in her favour with Moses and he intercedes before God, "Heal her, God!" (Num 12:11-13). The *Midrash* takes up this request literally and imagines that God himself heals her.

> The Holy One, blessed be he, said, "I am the priest, I set her apart and I declare her pure" (*Midrash* Deut 6:9)

Miriam will be healed, but not before seven days during which she is obliged to remain in isolation outside the encampment. Meanwhile, the march in the desert is halted:

> So Miriam was shut up outside the camp seven days; and the people did not set out on the march till Miriam was brought in again (Num 12:15).

This detail of the waiting for seven days on the part of the community is seen in the Judaic tradition as a further sign of the dignity of this extraordinary woman.

Therefore, even the narrative of Numbers 12, in itself negative, has been read in a perspective of exaltation. The importance of Miriam is such that everybody waits: from the people, to the priests, to the cloud (or rather, God himself). Miriam has merited to be 'awaited' as a reward for having waited on the banks of the Nile until the life of Moses was in safety:

29. I SENT BEFORE YOU MIRIAM (Mic 6:4)

Silver statuette from Kish, Iraq (VI century BC; Baghdad, Iraq Museum).

Miriam waited for her brother a while, as it is said, "And his sister stood afar off" (Ex 2:4). And in the wilderness God caused the ark, the *Shekinah*, the priests, all Israel and the seven clouds of glory to wait for her, as it is said, "And the people journeyed not till Miriam was brought in again", Num 12:15 (*Mekilta* of Rabbi Ishmael on Ex 16:35).

Miriam dies, and there is no water

The symbolism of the water from the well, to which reference has been made when speaking of Rachel, is closely linked also with the figure of Miriam. In fact, in the Haggadaic tradition the presence/absence of water is associated with the presence/absence of Miriam. As water was given through the merits of Miriam, so at her death the water fails. Such an association is made with Numbers 20:1-2 in mind. In itself the sacred text gives one notice after the other, without any intrinsic link:

> The people settle at Kadesh.
> There Miriam dies and is buried.
> Now there was no water for the community.

The first notice relates the death of the elder sister and can be compared with Numbers 20:24 and Deuteronomy 34:5, where the death of the other two great personages – Aaron and Moses – is recorded. The second notice introduces a new episode, known as 'the water of Meribah', that is, the waters of the dispute of strife (Num 20:2-13). But what for the Western reader and expert is abundantly clear, in the eyes of the Hebrew interpreter is not without subtle connections. In this particular case, since the water had been given through the merits of Miriam, it is seen to fail at her death. It is a case of symbolic reading, but not without interesting reflections:

> Since the well was given through the merits of Miriam, when she died the well was hidden and there was no more water for the community (*Targum* of Num 20:2).

Why was it that Israel, wandering in the desert, should have been given water because of Miriam? And why at her death did it fail? Miriam, as we have seen, is above all the prophetess – the one who speaks in the name of the Lord and with confidence awaits the fulfilment of what the Lord has announced through her.

She is the woman who trusts in the Lord, who hopes in his Word. Her faith permits the water to rise up, the water of divine revelation, the water of the Word that gives life to Israel during the journey in the desert towards the promised land. Miriam, therefore, cannot die without at the same time sealing off the supply of water for the community!

The rabbinic school teaches that Israel received three gifts through the merits of the three great figures of the Exodus: the well, by merit of Miriam; the column of cloud, by merit of Aaron; the manna, by merit of Moses. But these gifts were taken from Israel at the death of the three respective intermediaries: the well at the death of Miriam, the cloud when Aaron died and the manna at the death of Moses.

According to Rabbi Yehoshua b. Hananiah, the gifts of the water and the cloud were prolonged, thanks to the intercession of Moses. But who could intercede after his death?

> When Miriam died, the well was taken away. When Aaron died, the cloud of glory was taken away. When Moses died, the manna was taken away. Rabbi Joshua says, When Miriam died, the well was taken away, but it then came because of the merits of Moses and Aaron. When Aaron died, the cloud of glory was taken away, but it then came back because of the merits of Moses. When Moses died, all three, the well, the cloud of glory, and the manna were taken away and returned no more (*Mekilta* of Rabbi Ishmael on Ex 16:35).

It is to be hoped that they return with the advent of the new Moses, the Messiah!

A prophetic pastoral ministry

Moses and Miriam are presented to us even today as an inspiration for those who, in various ways, are called to collaborate for the human, social and religious formation of the people of God. Closely bound up with the experience of the exodus, their work is seen as important for every generation. In reality, it can be said that every generation is called to realize an exodus in its own collective history.

What significance and bearing does all this have for the life of the contemporary Church? The account of the exodus presents us with a paradigm of the various stages, or phases, of a process of liberation. The first thing that needs to happen is an awakening in the oppressed (the present-day slaves of the Pharaoh) of the faith that God is capable of changing even apparently hopeless situations. This expectant faith is certainly no 'opiate of the people'. It is bound up with struggle and commitment.

To lead one's brothers and sisters to freedom is burdensome: it requires patience, determination and courage. It means overcoming the various 'temptations' of the desert. However paradoxical it may seem, oppression succeeds in giving a measure of security, while liberty involves risk and adventure. It is not easy to unmask the false certainties advertised by the powers-that-be, that in our day are often found wearing the garments of consumerism, and re-awaken the sense of the dignity and worth of the human person.

The experiences of Moses and Miriam present a strong basis on which to build. There is the memory of the divine promises of the past, as a means of moulding people together in their diversity. This can then give birth to the consciousness of being one people, even to the point of attracting individuals to an encounter with the God of their fathers. They may even then choose to make him their God too, once and for all.

The pastoral work of liberation, originating with this wonderful couple of brother and sister, has the covenant as its goal. In actual fact, the scene of the covenant (Ex 24) reveals a rapport with God that embraces the recognition and solidarity existing among the various tribes. At the moment in which Israel becomes a people in the full sense of the word, at the foot of Mount Sinai, the differences among the various tribes do not disappear, but rather, each becomes represented individually, by its own carved stone pillar (stele). In other words, community is not realized to the detriment of the individual characteristics. Rather, it values the plurality of tradition and experiences, weaving them together into a wider framework made possible by the gracious initiative of God.

Israel, gathered together by Moses at the foot of Mount Sinai, is therefore an admirable figure of the Church of Jesus, not because it supplants the diversities, but because it welcomes the differences: "there is neither Jew nor Greek" (Gal 3:28). For he has made of the two into one (cf Eph 2:14-16), not a super-power, but a communion of communities.

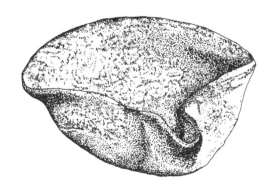

30. A LIGHT TO MY PATH (Ps 119:105)

Canaanite oil lamp in clay discovered at Tell Dor, Israel.

All this is extremely binding for the one who is placed before the people of God to lead them, but no less so, for all those baptized. In fact, the journey towards freedom found in the exodus must enable the people to walk in unity and develop solidarity as they go. The manna is gathered not only for themselves, but for all those who share the tent. The Word is listened to together, and the moral commitment it calls forth requires a common response, "All the people answered with one voice, and said, 'All the words which the Lord has spoken we will do'" (Ex 24:3).

Miriam, more than any other woman in the Old Testament, manifests a surprising gift of leadership, which not even the Rabbis (normally critical in this regard) have been able to ignore. Her activity reveals numerous subtleties: from her solicitude for and even criticism of the male leader (see Ex 2:4 and Num 12:1), to the prophetic interpretation of the intervention of God in history, to animating the celebration of liturgy. Miriam is capable of contributing beauty and attractiveness to the liturgical action and sweetening the water of the Word for the community to drink.

Thus Moses and Miriam display a complementarity in leading the people, a leadership which is shared by man and woman capable of teaching us to this day how to bring a people to enjoy the hospitality of God in his tent.

DAVID AND ABIGAIL

The Bible relates the story of David in a charming manner, giving expression to an obvious attraction for the common man become king, for the shepherd boy of Israel whom God chooses to shepherd Israel.

The traditions relating to this story are gathered principally from the two books of Samuel, continuing into 1 Kings 1 with the problem of the succession to the throne, and 1 Kings 2:1-10 with the testament and the death of David. Sources which mainly parallel 2 Samuel are found in 1 Chronicles 11-29.

As with the preceding figures of Jacob and Moses, we do not intend to deal with the problems of literary criticism or of tracing the history of the sources and traditions. We shall not be preoccupied with establishing which of the accounts is the most ancient, nor how the various sources were drawn together by the redactor. Our objective revolves around the text in its final form.

Our particular point of interest in the figure of David is the symbolic 'transposition' of his occupation: from guardian of the sheep of Jesse to leader (*nagid*) of Israel, and the fact that he is seen to be the paradigm of messianic hope. In actual fact, the double title shepherd-king, reconstructed from the tradition related to the story of David, offers, so to speak, historic roots to the messianic concept that developed around those two titles. The Messiah will be 'son of David' precisely in as much he will inherit his royal-pastoral rôle.

We shall place alongside David the figure of Abigail, the most important woman in his life, even if not as commonly known as Bathsheba, the object of irresistible lust and mother of the successor to the throne. However, in the Judaic tradition it is Abigail, and not Bathsheba, who appears in the historical quartet of the most beautiful women or, more importantly still, in the septet of the prophetesses of Israel.

The pastoral origins of David

The accounts in 1 Samuel underline a recurring biblical theme: the raising up of the lowly, the one who seemed destined to live and die as other men of his condition without making a mark in history. Instead, something unforeseen happens. The young shepherd of Bethlehem, reared between the hills and the desert of Judah, arrives in court, and the commoner reveals himself to be not only shrewd, but he is also a poet and musician. He is strong and handsome, humble and generous: it is he whom the prophet will consecrate *nagid*, leader of Israel!

Naturally, all this gives rise to folklore. People identify with this story. In some way, they find an interpretation for their personal lives. David comes from the conditions commonly shared by the greater part of the people (working-class) and so the people make him their hero. His amazing rise to power is seen as a singular blessing from God, who does not stop at appearances, but sees the heart.

The youngest of the sons of Jesse

We find the first account in 1 Samuel 16:1-13. Samuel must accept the new undertaking that the Lord has entrusted to him. Enough weeping for Saul! "How long will you grieve over Saul, seeing I have rejected him from being king over Israel? Fill your horn with oil, and go" (1 Sam 16:1).

The prophet has to go to Jesse of Bethlehem since it is from amongst his sons that Yahweh has chosen for himself a king. Samuel attempts to evade the issue (as Moses had done), not only because he is still attached to Saul, but also because his life is at stake: "If Saul hears it, he will kill me" (1 Sam 16:2).

To avoid arousing Saul's suspicion, the Lord proposes to give his journey a religious intent: "Take a heifer with you, and say, 'I have come to sacrifice to the Lord'. And invite Jesse to the sacrifice, and I will show you what you shall do; and you shall anoint for me him whom I name to you" (1 Sam 16:2-3).

The anointing of David, therefore, is seen to originate in the gracious choice of Yahweh. The continuation of the narrative demonstrates how that choice contradicts the traditional human standards, to the extent that even Samuel is taken by surprise. The sons of Jesse come in and immediately the eyes of Samuel rest on tall and robust Eliab. He probably reminds him of Saul, who is still dear to him. But the Lord dissuades him: "Do not look on his appearance or on the height of his stature, because I have rejected him; for the Lord sees not as man sees; man looks on the outward appearance, but the Lord looks on the heart" (1 Sam 16:7).

Jesse brings each of his sons before the prophet: Abinabad, the second-born, then Shammah and all the others: "And Jesse

31. FILL YOUR HORN WITH OIL (1 Sam 16:1)

Ivory vessel in the form of a horn (XIV century BC; Jerusalem, Rockefeller Archaeological Museum).

made seven of his sons pass before Samuel. And Samuel said to Jesse, 'The Lord has not chosen these'" (1 Sam 16:10).

Delusion clouds the face of Jesse. The feast, yet to begin, seems ended. The narrator does not say as much, but he allows us to sense it. And there is more! It would appear that the father is not even aware that he has another son – a direct question on the part of Samuel is needed to remind him:

> "Are all your sons here?" And he said, "There remains yet the youngest, but behold, he is keeping the sheep." And Samuel said to Jesse, "Send and fetch him; for we will not sit down till he comes here" (1 Sam 16:11).

David is the last son, 'the youngest' (*haqqatan*), the one who always risks being left out in the family decisions. As the last born, he is always seen as little, more to be protected than consulted (see 1 Sam 19:28-29). Jesse sends for him:

> Now he was ruddy, and had beautiful eyes, and was handsome. And the Lord said, "Arise, anoint him; for this is he."
>
> Then Samuel took the horn of oil, and anointed him in the midst of his brothers; and the Spirit of the Lord came mightily upon David from that day forward (1 Sam 16:12-13).

32. AND SAUL WAS SOOTHED (1 Sam 16:23)

Terracotta from Tell Asmar, Iraq (II millennium BC; Paris, Louvre Museum).

The shepherd-poet who plays the harp well

In 1 Samuel 16:14 there begins a narrative, independent from the one preceding it, probably belonging to a more ancient tradition. According to this account, David is summoned to the court of Saul, thanks to his power of speech and his talents as a musician. The information was offered by one of the young men at court:

> "Behold, I have seen a son of Jesse the Bethlehemite, who is skilful in playing, a man of valour, a man of war, prudent in speech, and a man of good presence; and the Lord is with him" (1 Sam 16:18).

This kind of presentation indicates the tangible sign of the divine blessing. Such diverse gifts are rarely found together in the same person. David is a poet but also a warrior; he can play well and speak well; he is young and handsome. Consequently God is with him: he is blessed by the Lord!

Saul immediately requests that he be brought to him and he makes him his armour-bearer:

> Therefore Saul sent messengers to Jesse, and said, "Send me David your son, who is with the sheep." And Jesse took an ass

laden with bread, and a skin of wine and a kid, and sent them by David his son to Saul.

And David came to Saul, and entered his service. And Saul loved him greatly, and he became his armour-bearer.

And Saul sent to Jesse, saying, "Let David remain in my service, for he has found favour in my sight."

And whenever the evil spirit from God was upon Saul, David took the lyre and played it with his hand; so Saul was refreshed, and was well, and the evil spirit departed from him (1 Sam 16:19-23).

David, lyre in hand, in ecstasy while composing and playing psalms, is one of the most favourite iconographic images, in both the Judaic and Christian traditions. As such, even the crusaders had him in mind when they christened the fortress of Herod 'David's stronghold', almost calling forth the melodious sound of his lyre on the heights of the holy city. They are hints of legend, but not far removed from the myth of David, the shepherd and poet, the warrior and harpist, present in the Bible.

The strong and brave shepherd who overpowers the lion

In 1 Samuel 17:12 we find the beginning of another narrative concerning David's so-called 'ascent to the throne'. The three elder brothers, Eliab, Abinadab and Shammah, were enrolled in the army of Saul which was engaged in battle against the Philistines; David, instead, was still young and 'came and went' (freely playing) between military service and the care of the flock.

The father sends him with provisions for his brothers and to collect their pay. David sets out, arrives, sees the giant provoking the Israelites and inquires, "What shall be done for the man who kills this Philistine, and takes away the reproach from Israel?" (1 Sam 17:26).

His brother Eliab overhears and immediately assumes his rôle of eldest brother, "Why have you come down? And with whom have you left those few sheep in the wilderness?" (1 Sam 17:28). David insists, "Can't one ask a question?". He moves away from Eliab, and continues his investigation with others. He is brought to Saul and, with astonishing courage, puts forward his proposal to confront Goliath:

"Your servant will go and fight with this Philistine."

And Saul said to David, "You are not able to go against this Philistine to fight with him; for you are but a youth, and he has been a man of war from his youth."

33. HE TOOK HIS SLING IN HIS HAND (1 Sam 17:40)

Canaanite slinger. Relief from the royal palace at Gozan, Syria (X-IX century BC; London, British Museum).

But David said to Saul, "Your servant used to keep sheep for his father; and when there came a lion, or a bear, and took a lamb from the flock, I went after him and smote him and delivered it out of his mouth; and if he arose against me, I caught him by his beard, and smote him and killed him. Your servant has killed both lions and bears; and this uncircumcised Philistine shall be like one of them, seeing he has defied the armies of the living God."

And David said, "The Lord who delivered me from the paw of the lion and from the paw of the bear, will deliver me from the hand of this Philistine" (1 Sam 17:32-37).

The rest is well known. Saul clothes the boy in his own armour, but with it David feels handicapped, unable to move. He removes it, putting on his own clothes. He takes the staff in his hand, slips five stones into his shepherd's bag and grasps the sling. And it is with this shepherd's catapult that he confronts and defeats Goliath (1 Sam 17:40-51).

Apart from the differences, the three accounts mentioned above agree in presenting the pastoral origins of David, his occupation and his experience as a shepherd. This is the basis which gives rise to the interpretation of his royalty, be it in the Bible or in the Judaic tradition. Yet before becoming king, when he was a fugitive in the desert of Judah, Scripture tells of a providential meeting with the wife of a rich shepherd, who was as beautiful as she was wise.

David had six wives, among whom was Michal, the beautiful daughter of Saul, who saved his life from the hand of her father. But the most important of his wives was Abigail, in whom – according to the Judaic tradition – were found together beauty, wisdom and gifts of prophecy.

Abigail the wise woman

Her intellectual ability reveals itself at the very first encounter when, notwithstanding the dramatic tension of the moment – the life of her husband and his entire household were in jeopardy – she handles the situation skilfully, assuming her husband's guilt and succeeding in dissuading David from justifying himself by the shedding of blood. Abigail does not save David from external dangers, but from himself, from the consequences of such a potentially disastrous action.

In the account of 1 Samuel 25, we are dealing with a David who was clearly exasperated by the unsettled life he was leading: on the boundaries of society and always on the defensive against the unforeseeable plots of Saul. Our hero had need of supplies to feed the starving men in his service.

News reaches him that Nabal, a wealthy owner of flocks, is shearing his sheep, and he takes advantage by sending his men

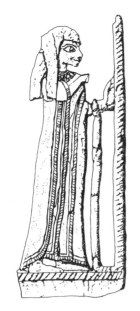

34. GO ON BEFORE ME, I WILL
FOLLOW YOU
(1 Sam 25:19)

Feminine Canaanite figure.
Ivory fragment discovered at
Megiddo (XIII-XII century BC;
Chicago, Oriental Institute Mu-
seum of University of Chicago).

to claim their share, on the basis of their so-called right of 'brotherhood': they had guaranteed a kind of protection to the shepherd of Nabal and it was only right that now they should be recompensed (1 Sam 25:7-9). But Nabal feels denied and humiliated, "Who is David? Who is the son of Jesse? There are many servants nowadays who are breaking away from their masters. Shall I take my bread and my water and my meat that I have killed for my shearers, and give it to men who come from I do not know where?" (1 Sam 25:10-11).

David reacts in an instant – Nabal must be eliminated. He gathers his men and sets off, determined to wipe out the entire family of Nabal.

The news quickly reaches Abigail. Without wasting time to reason with her husband (it would have been to no avail seeing he was so inconsiderate), the woman hurriedly prepares a rich assortment of provisions: "Then Abigail made haste, and took two hundred loaves, and two skins of wine, and five sheep ready dressed, and five measures of parched grain, and a hundred clusters of raisins, and two hundred cakes of figs, and laid them on asses" (1 Sam 25:18).

All this, with great solicitude, is sent ahead, as Jacob had done to regain Esau's good pleasure (Gen 32:14-22). She commands her servants, "'Go on before me; behold, I come after you'. But she did not tell her husband Nabal" (1 Sam 25:19). Abigail is a woman who knows what she is about, and can take risks.

The meeting

Abigail's meeting with David is described with statuesque detail: in the background, the austere suggestiveness of desert mountains that chase after one another like lambs of a flock (Ps 114:4). She descends from a hidden path, mounted on a donkey. Descending from the opposite height, he is brooding with anger and fury. "Now David had said, 'Surely in vain have I guarded all that this fellow has in the wilderness, so that nothing was missed of all that belonged to him; and he has returned me evil for good. God do so to David and more besides, if by morning I leave so much as one male of all who belong to him'" (1 Sam 25:21-22). As if by chance, the two meet face to face. Nimbly she springs from the saddle, prostrates herself on the ground and begins to speak:

"Upon me alone, my lord, be the guilt; pray let your handmaid speak in your ears, and hear the words of your handmaid. Let not my lord regard this ill-natured fellow, Nabal; for as his name is, so is he; Nabal is his name, and folly is with him; but I your

78

handmaid did not see the young men of my lord, whom you sent. Now then, my lord, as the Lord lives, and as your soul lives, seeing the Lord has restrained you from bloodguilt, and from taking vengeance with your own hand, now then let your enemies and those who seek to do evil to my lord be as Nabal. ...

For the Lord will certainly make my lord a sure house, because my lord is fighting the battles of the Lord; and evil shall not be found in you so long as you live. If men rise up to pursue you and to seek your life, the life of my lord shall be bound in the bundle of the living in the care of the Lord your God; and the lives of your enemies he shall sling out as from the hollow of a sling. And when the Lord has done to my lord according to all the good that he has spoken concerning you, and has appointed you prince over Israel, my lord shall have no cause of grief, or pangs of conscience, for having shed blood without cause or for my lord taking vengeance himself. And when the Lord has dealt well with my lord, then remember your handmaid" (1 Sam 25:24-31).

I think that nowhere else in Scripture do we find a discourse of such length placed on the lips of a woman. It is noteworthy particularly because in the biblical world, and more so in rabbinic tradition, even though wisdom is described in feminine terms, it is nevertheless predominantly incarnated in men. "A wise woman who can find?" (Prov 31:10). It is considered a rarity! But God allows David, the man who fears him, to meet such a woman.

The wisdom in not seeking revenge

The words of Abigail contain a lesson that a king and every son of Israel should never forget: that of placing one's cause in God's hands, rather than acting as judge in the situation. Saul had stubbornly resisted learning such a lesson, and David was about to fall into the same trap, in spite of his former show of magnanimity when he had rejected the opportunity to kill Saul, goaded on by his men who wanted him to take advantage of the situation. "Here is the day of which the Lord said to you, 'Behold, I will give your enemy into your hand, and you shall do to him as it shall seem good to you'" (1 Sam 24:4). On that occasion David limited himself to cutting off a corner of Saul's robe, and immediately felt remorse in his heart for having failed to show respect towards the Lord's anointed one (1 Sam 24:5-8).

David gives proof of his magnanimity on another occasion, when Saul lay sleeping in the camp with his sword stuck in the ground. Even then he resisted the temptation to kill him: "The Lord forbid that I should put forth my hand against the Lord's anointed!" (1 Sam 26:11).

35. SHE IS FAR MORE
PRECIOUS THAN JEWELS
(Pr 31:10)

Head of a Jewish woman in ivory (IX-VIII century BC; Israel, private collection).

In the two accounts which respectively precede and follow the meeting with Abigail, the sacred author shows the righteousness of David and the nobility of his soul. He refuses to vindicate himself against his enemy and commends his cause to the Lord. But in the case of Nabal, David does not seem to be guided by the forbearance shown to Saul. He is taken up with his own wounded pride that demands justice, with the offence that cries for vengeance.

The one who saves him in this fatal hour is a woman "who opens her mouth with wisdom", like the woman praised in Proverbs 31.

Beautiful, and above all, wise

Abigail is the woman who knows how to turn the heart of David to re-evaluate the situation with good sense and right judgement. To achieve her purpose she could have employed all her feminine powers of seduction: she had all the charm to captivate David's heart. Nevertheless, she does not sway him with her beauty but with the force of her wisdom.

David is enchanted and exclaims with emotion:

> "Blessed be the Lord, the God of Israel, who sent you this day to meet me!
> Blessed be your discretion, and blessed be you, who have kept me this day from bloodguilt and from avenging myself with my own hand!
> For as surely as the Lord the God of Israel lives, who has restrained me from hurting you, unless you had made haste and come to meet me, truly by morning there had not been left to Nabal so much as one male" (1 Sam 25:32-34).

According to Rabbi Samuel the good done by Abigail to David surpasses that of the ritual sacrifices, since it withheld him from committing a sin the sacrifices would not have been able to expiate:

> Endless is the good of a good woman. (...) R. Samuel taught: Abigail did more good for David than all the sacrifices in the world. For had David done that deed which he thought to do upon Nabal, then, even if David had brought all the sacrifices in the world, they would not have atoned for him. But Abigail came to him and saved him.... Even as sacrifices bring about forgiveness, Abigail brought about forgiveness [*mehilah*] for David (*Midrash* Ps 53:1).

Abigail among the prophetesses

The Judaic tradition numbers Abigail among the prophetesses of Israel, although the Scriptures reserve this title for only three women: Miriam, Deborah and Hulda. What did Abigail do to merit such an honour?

The Rabbis bring to light the subtlety of her reasoning and her gifts as a prophetess. Besides predicting that David will become king in place of Saul, as is found in the biblical text (1 Sam 25:30), they imply that Abigail also foresees the sin with Bathsheba: to this would refer the words: "my lord shall have no cause of grief" (1 Sam 25:31).

In a fine dialogue, conducted with argumentative skill and coquettish allusions, Abigail moves from the menstrual blood of the woman to the blood of judgement, that is to say, the problem of the sentence of death that David had pronounced against her husband together with all his family.

Blessed be your discretion

"And it was so, as she rode on her ass and came down by the covert of the mountain..."

"By the covert [*sether*] of the mountain"? It should say "from the mountain"!

Rabbah b. Samuel said, It means that she came with reference to blood that came from the hidden parts [*setharim*]. She brought some blood and showed it to him. He said to her, "Is blood to be shown by night"? She replied, "Are capital cases tried at night?"

He said to her, "He [Nabal] is a rebel against the king, and no trial is necessary for him".

She replied, "Saul is still alive, and your fame is not yet spread abroad in the world".

Then he said to her, "Blessed be thy discretion and blessed be thou that hast kept me this day from blood-guiltiness".

The word *damim* [blood-guiltiness] is plural, to indicate two kinds of blood. The passage teaches that she bared her thigh and he went three parasangs by the light of it.

He said, "Listen to me". She replied, "Let not this be a stumbling-block to thee".

The word 'this' implies that something else would be, and what was that? The incident of Bathsheba; and so it was eventually.

(*Babylonian Talmud,* Megillah, 14a-b)

According to a rabbinic interpretation, Abigail develops a complex argument around a double sense of blood: that of a woman's menstruation and that of a vendetta. Besides the wisdom of the woman, the text gives evidence of her recourse to the weapons of seduction and calculation in order to convince David to choose magnanimity.

In this sense, Abigail uses the weapon of her feminine seductiveness to put pressure on David to dissuade him from taking a decision in haste regarding the slaughter he has in mind. She does not deny her feminine wiles, but employs them to a good end, contrary to Bathsheba, the other seductive woman in David's life, who brought him sin and death (2 Sam 11).

The courage to share a vagrant life

Returning home, Abigail found her husband feasting in great style, incapable of understanding the situation and ignorant of the impending danger, like the generation of Noah on the eve of the flood. "And Nabal's heart was merry within him, for he was very drunk; so she told him nothing at all until the morning light. And in the morning, when the wine had gone out of Nabal, his wife told him these things, and his heart died within him, and he became as a stone. And about ten days later the Lord smote Nabal; and he died" (1 Sam 25:36-38).

David interprets what follows as an intervention of justice on the part of the Lord. He blesses God for having restrained himself from doing what was evil, so he sends messengers to Abigail with the request that she become his wife.

She is still at Carmel, where the shearing of the flock had taken place. Probably she had responsibility for the administration of the household and property, as is written of the wise woman in Proverbs 31. By marrying her, David would acquire her patrimony in livestock (3,000 sheep and 1,000 goats), which constituted a fair gain for him, constrained as he was to provide for so many men in precarious conditions. But what of her?

At that time David was still a fugitive, living on the boundaries of society, the head of a mob of plunderers, not the king of Israel. In fact, a phrase in Abigail's discourse leads us to understand that she foresees David's success and declares herself available: "remember your handmaid!". This phrase make her appear flirtatious in the eyes of the Rabbis, who observe that the title 'servant' is not assumed by a married woman. If this is so, the offer of marriage on the part of David would come as a crown upon the dream of the woman.

However, let us reflect on what it means for Abigail to accept David's proposal. It means leaving the security of her property to share a life of wandering and of constant peril. Scripture points out that she followed him to Gat, the country of the Philistines (1 Sam 27:3) and then to Hebron (2 Sam 2:2), where she gave birth to Kileab (2 Sam 3:3). So Abigail manifests courage and great determination in confronting hardships, sustained by her faith in David and in the God who protects him.

It is in Hebron, the city which is associated with the memory of the patriarchs, that David is officially consecrated king, first over the house of Judah (2 Sam 2:4) and then also over the tribes of the North (2 Sam 5:1-3). His consecration as king of Judah is recounted very briefly. David had already earned the respect of his tribe, which had no difficulty in accepting him. On the other hand, recognition from the tribes of the North came only after many hard and long vicissitudes, which resulted in the decimation of the house of Saul.

The declaration of the tribes of the North expresses, in the first place, a bond of kinship acquired with David: "Behold, we are your bone and flesh" (2 Sam 5:1), just as a husband united with his wife forms with her a single reality. They acknowledge his rôle as leader, recalling the success of his enterprises as commander of Israel while Saul was still alive. However, what strikes us most is that precisely from the mouths of the Northen tribes we find the designation of the rôle of the king in pastoral terms:

> The Lord said to you, "You shall be shepherd of my people Israel, and you shall be prince over Israel" (2 Sam 5:2).

The matter is anything but fortuitous; in fact, as we shall see in greater depth, it is there in the religious tradition of the North that this terminology of the shepherd is rooted and transmitted (see the Psalms of Asaf).

Consequently, in offering to David their political submission, the elders do not forget the religious dimension: they connect the royalty with the experience of the patriarchs and the nomadic tradition of the people.

An explicit correlation between the juvenile occupation of David and his appointment as king is found in the words that God addresses to him from the lips of Nathan:

> I took you from the pasture, from following the sheep, that you should be prince (*nagid*) over my people Israel (2 Sam 7:8).

This relationship has profoundly affected the memory of Israel. There is a beautiful example of it in Psalm 78 where, following one upon the other, are the memory of David's original occupation and his call to shepherd and guide Israel:

He chose David his servant,
and took him from the sheepfolds;
from tending the ewes that had young he brought him
to be the shepherd of Jacob his people,
of Israel his inheritance.

With upright heart he tended them,
and guided them with skilful hand (Ps 78:70-72).

Taking this psalm as a starting point, the *Midrash* argues that God puts his just ones to the test, giving them a flock to pasture, as was the case with Moses. In what sense did David pass the test? According to the *Midrash*, when he was in the desert, it was his custom to nourish the sheep according to their needs. He led the smallest ones out of the fold first, having reserved the tender grass for them. The larger sheep were left to eat the ordinary grass, and the robust sheep and goats were satisfied with the tougher grass. And God said:

> "He who knows how to look after sheep, bestowing upon each the care it deserves, shall come and tend my people", as it says: "From following the ewes that give suck He brought him, to be sheperd over Jacob his people", Psalm 78:71 (Ex R. 2:2).

The transfer of the ark and the dance of David

With the conquest of Jerusalem, which becomes his city, David had attained a degree of stability in government and he desired to bind the young kingdom to the religious tradition of Israel, in particular to the tent and the ark. The tent

---

I was the smallest

Composed in the second, or perhaps the third century BC, this psalm, which was known in its Greek (Septuagint) and Syriac versions, was found in the original Hebrew at Qumran. It can be considered as a poetic midrash concerning chapters 16 and 17 of 1 Samuel.

I was the smallest,
I was the smallest among
  my brothers,
and the youngest among the
  sons of my father;
and he made me shepherd
  of his flocks,
and the ruler over his kids.
(...)
He sent his prophet to
  anoint me,
Samuel to make me great;
my brothers went out to
  meet him,
handsome of figure and
  handsome of appearance.

(Although) their stature was
  tall,
(and) their hair handsome,
the Lord God did not choose
  them.
But he sent and took me
  while tending the flock,
and he anointed me with
  holy oil,
And he made me leader for
  his people
and ruler over the sons of
  his covenant.

(11 QPs 151)

indicated the presence of Yahweh who had made himself a bedouin with his people in the desert. The ark evoked a presence reminiscent of the warrior, for by it Yahweh had guided the children of Israel in their battles for the conquest and overthrow of the Canaanite people. David, therefore, desired to transfer the ark to his own city and install it as the victorious presence of the Lord in the tent specially prepared for it.

After the glorious feats of Joshua (Josh 4-6), the ark of the Lord had fallen into the hands of the Philistines (1 Sam 4:11). The shock suffered by all the people on that occasion is dramatically demonstrated by the elderly Eli, who died instantly on receiving the news (1 Sam 4:18). However, the Lord took it upon himself to restore his own dignity: the ark produced terrible scourges among the Philistines, who felt constrained to return it with gifts of appeasement (1 Sam 5-6).

To these events is linked the initiative of David to transport the ark of the Lord from Kiriat-Yearin to Jerusalem (2 Sam 6). Two attempts were necessary, however, before the ark could take its place under the tent in the city of David. The first ended tragically: Yahweh caused Uzzah to die, angry at him for having placed his hand on the ark to steady it on the cart, while the oxen hauled it over uneven ground. The second attempt was successful: the ark was transported by Levites, as the law prescribed (1 Chron 15:26), and not carted by oxen as previously, in imitation of the Philistines (1 Sam 6:7-8).

The transfer of the ark assumed the rite of a solemn procession in which David acted not so much as king, but rather as a priest and charismatic leader of the entourage: "and when those who bore the ark of the Lord had gone six paces, he sacrificed an ox and a fatling. And David danced before the Lord with all his might; and David was girded with a linen ephod. So David and all the house of Israel brought up the ark of the Lord with shouting, and with the sound of the horn" (2 Sam 6:13-15).

The only discordant note was voiced by Michal, the wife of David. This proud heiress of the house of Saul shows indignation at David's behaviour: "How the king of Israel honoured himself today, uncovering himself today before the eyes of his servants' maids, as one of the vulgar fellows shamelessly uncovers himself!" (2 Sam 6:20). But David is so full of gratitude to the Lord for having chosen him that he sees nothing improper: "It was before the Lord, who chose me above your father, and above all his house, to appoint me as prince over Israel, the people of the Lord – and I will make merry before the Lord. I will make myself yet more contemptible than this, and I will be abased in your eyes; but by the maids of whom you have spoken, by them I shall be held in honour" (2 Sam 6:21-22).

These words are an indication of David sentiments. Even

The ark of the covenant. The entrance stone of the synagogue of Capernaum, Israel (IV-V century AD).

after numerous victories, his heart is still filled with wonder, because when he was a young shepherd he was chosen to take the place of the great Saul. Installing the ark of the Lord under the tent in his own city is for him an occasion of thanksgiving. But also, the style is important: just as God, so to speak, did 'crazy' things for him, so he too feels the need to 'let himself go' for God before the eyes of all. He is convinced that it will not bring him shame, but rather honour; and especially from the 'servants of his servants': of the women belonging to his ministers and to the people, whom he maintains to be the most understanding of all.

The Lord will build a house for you

Since Israel had taken possession of the land they no longer lived in tents but in houses, and David, already at the height of power, owned the largest and most beautiful one. Now he feels ill at ease living "in a house of cedar, while the ark of God dwells in a tent" (2 Sam 7:2), and he makes known his intention to construct a temple.

The prophet Nathan, informed of the king's plan, affirms and encourages him; but Yahweh during the night sends a message that tells David to abandon his plan. The motive for the refusal lies in the choice that the Lord had made to share, at all times, the precarious conditions in which the people live, rather than the comfortable lifestyle of the king. The words of Yahweh also betray a controversial note:

I have not dwelt in a house since the day I brought up the people of Israel from Egypt to this day, but I have been moving about in a tent for my dwelling.

In all places where I have moved with all the people of Israel, did I speak a word with any of the judges of Israel, whom I commanded to shepherd my people Israel, saying, "Why have you not built me a house of cedar?" (2 Sam 7:6-7).

However, the Lord appreciates David's intention. What is more, he announces an amazing reversal of plans:

Would you build me a house to dwell in? ...

Moreover the Lord declares to you that the Lord will make you a house.

... I will raise up your offspring after you, who shall come forth from your body, and I will establish his kingdom. He shall build a house for my name, and I will establish the throne of his kingdom for ever (2 Sam 7:5, 11-13).

This great promise of the Lord, which constitutes a special covenant with the house of David does not conceal the fact that the impossibility of constructing the temple implies a certain obscuring of the figure of David. The author of the second Book of Chronicles tries in some way to make amends by narrating that before his death the king prepared all the building material for the construction of the temple and encouraged his young son Solomon to bring it to completion without delay (1 Chron 29:1-9).

A glorified royalty

In the Judaic tradition, the figure of David undoubtedly occupies a prime position side by side with the greatest personages of Israel. For example, to exalt the multiple aspects of his works, the *Midrash* on the Psalms likens him to Moses, the greatest of the prophets:

The foremost among prophets – he is Moses, of whom it is said *And Moses went up unto God* (Ex 19:3); the foremost among kings – he is David. You find that whatever Moses did, David did.

As Moses led Israel out of Egypt, so David led Israel out of servitude to Goliath. As Moses fought the battles of the Lord against Sihon and Og, so David fought the battles of the Lord in all the regions around him, as Abigail said: *My lord fighteth the battles of the Lord* (1 Sam 25:28).

As Moses became king in Israel and in Judah, for it is said *And he became king in Ieshurun, when the heads of the people ... were gathered together* (Deut 33:5), so David became king in Israel and in Judah.

As Moses divided the Red Sea for Israel, so David divided the rivers of Aram for Israel, as it is said *David ... divided the rivers of Aram* (Ps 60:1, 2).

As Moses built an altar, so David built an altar.

As the one brought offerings, so the other brought offerings.

As Moses gave five books of laws to Israel, so David gave five books of psalms to Israel... (*Midrash* Ps 1:2).

The Rabbis have resolved the problem of David's failure to build the temple by having recourse to Psalm 30 which bears the following heading: 'Song for the dedication of the temple of David'. This is a beautiful text, in which what could have appeared as a blemish on the figure of the king, is transformed by them into a reason for exaltation. If David had constructed the temple it would have been indestructible, while instead, the Holy One had already foreseen its destruction for the salvation of the children of Israel:

Though David deserved to build the house, the prophet Nathan came and said to David, "Thou shalt not build a house unto My name, because thou hast shed much blood upon the earth in My sight" (1 Chron 22: 22-8).

When David heard this, he was afraid, and he said, "Behold, I am unfit to build the Temple." According to R. Judah bar Llai, the Holy One, blessed be he, said to David, "David, be not afraid." (…)

David then asked God, "If this is so, why am I not allowed to build the Temple?"

The Holy One, blessed be he, replied, "If thou build the Temple, behold! it will stand and abide and never be destroyed."

David said, "But that is as it should be!"

The Holy One, blessed be he, answered, "It is revealed and known unto Me that the children of Israel will sin, and then I shall cool the fire of My fury upon the Temple and destroy it, and only thus will the children of Israel be saved (…)

The Holy One, blessed be he, also said to David, "Even if thous art not to build the Temple, nevertheless, since thou didst think to build it, I shall record it in thy name," as is said, "A song at the dedication of the house of David" (Ps 30:1): Scripture does not say "the house of Solomon" but "the house of David". Why? Because David thought in his heart to build the temple. Thus we learn that when a man thinks of doing a good work, even if he is prevented from doing it, the Holy One, blessed be he, reckons it as though he had done it (*Midrash* Ps 62:4).

One aspect associated with the sanctuary is the poetic and musical activity of David. In composing psalms, he most eminently fulfils his rôle as leader. He does this not only in the military and political sense, but also religiously, for the glorification of God who had chosen him, and for the formation of the people entrusted to his care:

> David said, "I will sing on account of the glory which thou hast given me, as is said *Who am I, O Lord God, and what is my house, that thou hast brought me hither?* (2 Sam 7:18) – that is, brought me to my kingship. (...) Therefore I have not been sleeping, but have awaked the dawn with psaltery and harp, as it is said, Awake, *psaltery and harp, I will awake the dawn* (Ps 108:3)." David went on, "Never has dawn come upon me and found me asleep. For I am wont to awake the dawn" (*Midrash* Ps 108:2-3).

And the rich man carried away the poor man's only sheep...

The idealization of the figure of David does not mean that his faults are concealed or camouflaged. Now, among David's sins, the most notable is certainly his relationship with Bathsheba and the killing of Uriah.

The narrative is introduced in an unusual manner. There is no cause for a war, as in 2 Samuel 10. All that remains to be said is the time element: it was "the time when kings were wont to

---

Let me dwell in your tent

David said this, "*Let me dwell in thy tent for ever*" (Ps 61:5).

Could the thought have come into David's mind that he would live for ever?

If not, what is meant by 'for ever'?

According to Rabbi Judah, it means that David prayed, "For ever may my psalms be sung in houses of prayer and in houses of study".

The Holy One, blessed be he, replied, "Though thou wilt die, thy name shall never move from within my house", for psalms beginning *Psalm of David* shall be sung in thy name at every sacrifice. Nay more: Because thou didst consider building a sanctuary, which Solomon thy son shall build, I shall write its dedication in thy name, as is said *A Psalm and song at the dedication of the house of David* – not 'of Sol-omon', says Scripture, 'but of David'.

(*Midrash* Ps 30:4)

The memory of David lives on always through his psalms.

38. HE SAW A WOMAN
BATHING (2 Sam 11:2)

*Phoenician statuette in clay
from Achzib, Israel (XII century BC; Jerusalem, Rockefeller
Archaeological Museum).*

go to war". It is a far cry from the days when David went out at the head of his army to fight the battles of the Lord. He has since grown rich and powerful. He can afford to pay soldiers to wage wars of political expansion. So he sends Joab and all of Israel to devastate the country of the Ammonites, while he remains in the royal place in Jerusalem.

It was a late afternoon. David had had a prolonged rest. Perhaps he had eaten a large lunch. Rising from his bed on that late afternoon, he begins to take a stroll on the terrace of his palace. From there he sees a woman taking a bath. Probably she, too, is on the terrace of her house, much lower than that of the king, thus enabling him to see her. She was very beautiful. David does not think twice. He sends a servant to find out who she might be: she is the wife of Uriah, the Hittite, a foreign mercenary (the Hittites came from Asia Minor). David has her brought to him. His harem was certainly not lacking in beautiful women, above all there was Abigail. But now David wants this one and it is speedily accomplished: "So David sent messengers, and took her; and she came to him, and he lay with her" (2 Sam 11:4).

No words pass between them. But after some weeks the woman speaks. She sends word to him saying, "I am pregnant". Now David has to find a solution to save his face. He sends for Uriah to inform him about the condition of Joab and the progress of the war; then he invites him to go home to refresh himself. But Uriah must have been no fool. It must have already sounded strange to him that the king would choose him to inform himself of the progress of the war, and now this insistent offer of rest. Neither could he have been particularly well known at court if the king, up to this time, had never seen his wife. He sniffs suspicion in the air and instead of going down to his house, he passes the night at the portals of the palace.

Naturally, David is immediately informed and poor Uriah is once again summoned, "Have you not come from a journey? Why did you not go down to your house?" (2 Sam 11:10). The reply is extremely profound and touching to David's ears, "The ark and Israel and Judah dwell in booths; and my lord Joab and the servants of my lord are camping in the open field; shall I then go to my house, to eat and to drink, and to lie with my wife? As you live, and as your soul lives, I will not do this thing" (2 Sam 11:11).

If Uriah had suspected the plot, his reply would have been even more appreciable. He is a man of sterling character, a real comrade. He cannot indulge himself in rest and recreation when the others are risking their lives! His solidarity is truly extraordinary since, when all is said and done, he is a foreigner. And yet this Hittite is more loyal to Israel than the king himself.

He does not accept sleeping in his own bed while the ark, Israel and Judah dwell 'in tents'.

These words, so touching, fail nonetheless to reach the heart of David. Luxury and lust win the day: "Remain here today also". He invited him to dine and saw to it that he drank excessively, but not even then did Uriah go down to his own house that evening.

Then David precipitates a solution. The man before him is not insolent like Nabal, but Uriah's dedication is no less offensive: he openly condemns the sin and the meanness of the king, like the just man quoted in the Book of Wisdom, who with his very behaviour "reproaches those who transgress the law" (Wis 2:12). And, like the foolish in the Book of Wisdom, David eliminates the just: Uriah is positioned in the front line and then abandoned to his fate.

When the days of mourning for the husband had ended, David had Bathsheba brought to him. The matter now seemed resolved. The only impediment had been removed and even Joab, thanks to that death, had been spared the anger of the king (2 Sam 11:18-25). "But [comments the sacred author dryly] the thing that David had done displeased the Lord" (2 Sam 11:27).

Then who should present himself at the palace but Nathan, the prophet. He has a case to submit to the king:

> There were two men in a certain city, the one rich and the other poor. But the poor man had nothing but one little ewe lamb, which he had bought. And he brought it up, and it grew up with him and with his children; it used to eat of his morsel, and drink from his cup, and lie in his bosom, and it was like a daughter to him. Now there came a traveller to the rich man, and he was unwilling to take one of his own flock or herd to prepare for the wayfarer who had come to him, but he took the poor man's lamb, and prepared it for the man who had come to him (2 Sam 12:1-4).

Nathan's case is a beautiful parable that evokes youthful memories of David's early environment, his pastoral origins. It is especially devised to open a breach in David's sentiments, reawakening profound emotions. In fact, it turns out to be the perfect trap. What is best in David quickly comes to the surface: by his indignation he expresses a strong involvement in the case, and a sensitivity for justice which borders on the excessive: "As the Lord lives, the man who has done this deserves to die" (2 Sam 12:5). Ironically, the sentence rebounds upon himself, "You are that man".

The Judaic tradition is more lenient than Scripture and tends to reinstate David, giving emphasis to the continuation

39. SHOW ME THE WONDERS OF YOUR LOVE (Ps 17:7)

Gold buckles and rings found in the excavations of Beth Eglayim, Tel el-Aggul, Israel (II millennium BC).

of the narrative which promises forgiveness and the birth of Solomon:

> And David was distressed about his taking of Bathsheba, for men were speaking against him in Israel and saying, "Is it possible that he who took the ewe lamb, murdered its shepherd, and caused the people of Israel to die by the sword can ever have help from God?"
>
> But the Holy One, blessed be he, set his mind at rest, for Nathan said to David, "The Lord also hath put away thy sin; thou shalt not die" (2 Sam. 12:13).
>
> About the third matter, Israel said, "What does David think? That his kingship can be continued through Bathsheba's son?" But the Holy One, blessed be he, set David's mind at rest, for the word of the Lord came to David, saying, "Behold, a son shall be born to thee, who shall be a man of rest... his name shall be Solomon" (1 Chron 22:9).
>
> Concerning this verse, Rabbi Judah the Levite said, "Are not all sons born to their fathers? Why should Scripture say here born to thee? Because to thee means to heal thee – that is, to heal thee of thy sin" (*Midrash* Ps 4:2).

Another *Midrash* underlines the greatness of God's pardon and how there is no sin that cannot be forgiven if the sinner converses humbly with the Holy One, as David did:

> Have mercy upon me, O God, according to Thy loving-kindness (Ps 51:3).
>
> With whom may David be compared? With a man who had a wound on his hand and went to a physician. The physician said, "Thou canst not have treatment. The wound is large, but the money in this hand is little".
>
> The man said, "I beg thee, take all the money that I have here, and as for the rest, let it come from thee. Have mercy upon me, have compassion upon me".
>
> So, too, David said to the Holy One, blessed be he: "Have mercy upon me, O God, according to thy loving-kindness. Thou art compassionate and according to the multitude of thy compassions blot out my transgressions.
>
> Thou hast already shown me much mercy". David also said, "Show me the wonders of thy mercy, O thou that savest... them that take refuge in thee (Ps 17:7): healing comes from thee. Because the wound is large, lay on a large poultice for me, as is said: Wash me thoroughly from mine iniquity (Ps 51:4).
>
> Hence you learn that every man who knows that he has sinned, and prays because of his sin, and is in fear because of it, and holds converse about it with the Holy One, blessed be he, him the Holy One, blessed be he, forgives (*Midrash* Ps 51:2).

In conclusion, David proves to be a king, a warrior – never a diplomat. He is a leader in the full sense of the term: first in everything, in war and in love, in revenge and in magnanimity, in sin and in repentance. In all this he has only one preoccupation: never to obscure the all-surpassing strength, goodness and mercy of his Lord, as is wonderfully evidenced in his *Miserere*.

What can the couple David-Abigail propose to the life of the contemporary Church?

A pastoral style of government

David personifies clearly the qualities of leadership in all its dimensions. He does not inherit royal power by nature, he receives it as gift; but he also prepares for it by means of hard and humble apprenticeship which refines his natural talents. He reveals his sensitivity whether in the use of military power, or in caring for his people, in the administration of justice and the composition of song and poetry. He manifests a strong bond with the tradition of faith to which he intends to secure his kingdom. His religiosity is spontaneous and direct, devoid of formalism and conventions: just think that he watches and fasts when his infant son is ill, but perfumes himself and partakes of food when he dies.

He is a leader who does not allow power to make him rigid. Many of his faults are overlooked because of his great humanity. In some moments it would even seem that he transcends himself and becomes transparent to the divine pathos, the passionate care of God for mankind. For example, when they brought him the news that his son, Absalom, the would-be usurper of the throne and the violator of his women, had been killed. They counted on bringing him good news, but instead provoked a cry of anguish: "Absalom, my son Absalom, would that I had died instead of you", a cry which certainly does not echo reasons of state, but only the sentiments of a father, and furthermore, those of God.

This is the shepherd David that the Bible presents as a model for a leader of the people. Not a superman, and neither an ascetic nor a puritan. Rather, a blend of greatness and fragility, held together by what the Bible defines as a heart of integrity because it is strongly passionate towards Yahweh and his people.

Abigail's contribution to this model is that she is the wise woman that God placed at a crucial moment of David's life. Abigail remained a companion – and presumably a counsellor – throughout the years that followed. From her, David learns a most important lesson: not to pass judgement oneself, but to commend all judgements to the Lord. The figure of Abigail reminds us that leaders cannot permit themselves to make hasty decisions, dictated by fleeting sentiments, and that power should always go hand-in-hand with moderation and magnanimity.

Undoubtedly, the royal dimension of biblical pastoral care is that most exposed to misinterpretation, for it projects a theocratic vision of the world which is far removed from Western thinking. Already in biblical times, the figure of the king was perceived in contrast to the traditional ideal of equality among the tribes and their common subjection to Yahweh. To this end, one of the primary mandates of the prophet seems to be the function of control, in order that the rights of the king do not impinge upon those of the people and of the Lord. Ezekiel, in particular, as we shall see in the following chapter, shows concern for the exploitation threatened by the king. His intention is to redirect the king's power by a renewal of the pastoral vision.

The placing of emphasis on power while forgetting the function of pastoral care, has led to abuses of the royal office, be this in biblical times or those closer to our own day. On the other hand, the confusion between the two dimensions has given rise to a theocratic conception of power that has diminished the dignity of the people. Finally, modern culture has defined a neat distinction of rôles between the religious and political spheres, a distinction that, in the broadest sense of the term, has become divisive and has produced ruptures in the fabric of society.

The biblical perspective of pastoral care, with all its various components, suggests that distinctions should not become disparate, because the well-being of humanity is indivisible. The various people and institutions entrusted with leadership are meant to collaborate to achieve this well-being. By working together, in different ways, they can render visible the pastoral care of God for all humanity.

40. WITH UPRIGHT HEART HE SHEPHERDED THEM (Ps 78:72)

A gazelle. Fragment of polychromic parietal decoration from the tomb of Pharaoh Iti at el-Gebelin, Egypt (XXI century BC).

BEYOND HISTORY

Prophecy and Song

EXODUS
BETWEEN MEMORY AND PROPHECY

The experience of the exodus is undoubtedly the focal point of Scripture. This is evident from the fact that it goes beyond history and pervades prophecy and the spirituality of Israel. Some prophets love to evoke the memory of it by returning to the familiar and archaic metaphor of the shepherd, which they enrich with new symbolic meanings. The image is used to illustrate the mutual affection and trust between Yahweh and his people, and also the dramatic situation looming on the horizon: the deportation and exile to Babylon.

About 20 verbs, many of which are never applied to the divine shepherd in the neighbouring cultures, revolve around the figure and the task of the shepherd. For example, in Mesopotamian and Egyptian texts there is no mention that the divine shepherd had searched for and liberated his flock, nor that he had taken a firm stand against the shepherds appointed to pastor it. Biblical language can express itself in that way because it witnesses to and narrates a history that has no precedents, a history that is the foundation of Israel's true identity: the exodus.

In the Prophets, the exodus is constantly used as a yardstick and paradigm of what is read. The many vicissitudes and situations of the people of God are interpreted in the light of the first and fundamental experience in which God reveals himself as a shepherd who saves and sets free.

Hosea, one of the most ancient of the prophetic writers (eighth century BC) carried out his ministry in the northern region of the country in a period of strong social disparity. In contrast to the prosperity and well-being of some families pertaining to the ruling classes, there was the poverty of the majority. The economy depended on agriculture as its main resource, thanks to a higher rainfall in comparison to Judea.

In this agricultural environment a strong hold was exercised

HOSEA

In their pastures they have satisfied themselves and forgotten me

41. I WILL TAKE FROM HER
MOUTH THE NAMES OF
THE BAALS (Hos 2:17)

The god Baal Hadad standing on a bull. Bass-relief in limestone from Amrit, Syria (VI century BC; Paris, Louvre Museum).

by the Canaanite rites of fertility, bound up with the god Baal and his consort Astartes. Unlike Yahweh, who could neither be seen nor touched, Baal was a god within reach: he could be represented and his statuettes were part of everyday life. His festivals marked the seasons, in a cycle involving life, death and resurrection. In this way, the worship of Baal inserted the believer into the life-giving cycle of nature. These rites were certainly more attractive than the Israelite feast of shelters with its atmosphere of austerity. The concurrent Canaanite feast of the harvest, where the songs of the reapers and sheaf-bearers were interspersed with choruses and sacred dances, must have held a strong fascination for the Israelites.

Into this milieu Hosea is sent, charged with the mission of reclaiming the people from the seductions of idolatry. How was he to inspire the people to summon up the strength of will that would enable them to overcome the seductions of the fertility rites? The prophet draws inspiration from the past. To the fertile land of Canaan he contrasts the desert, with its scorched and barren earth. It is there that for 40 years Yahweh had surrounded his people with solicitude and affection, as a young man for his loved one. Israel must return to this first love: "I will allure her, and bring her into the wilderness, and speak tenderly to her. And there she shall answer as in the days of her youth, as at the time when she came out of the land of Egypt" (Hos 2:14-15).

The love of Israel, however, is fickle and rebellious:

Like a stubborn heifer, Israel is stubborn;
can the Lord now feed them
like a lamb in a broad pasture? (Hos 4:16).

The patient pastoral care of the Lord is sorely tried by the stubbornness of the people. The prophet is obliged to incarnate the persistence of the love of God that overcomes infidelity and betrayal, by marrying a prostitute. But the woman remains unfaithful, like the people. It is difficult, at this point, to separate the behaviour of the prophet from that of God. One thing, however, is certain: the prophet (and the lover – God) devises every strategy, even to strewing the path with thorns until the loved one no longer runs after other lovers and in the end is compelled to say, "I will go and return to my first husband, for it was better with me then than now" (Hos 2:7).

The Lord is prepared to try anything to win back the heart of Israel. He transforms himself from the shepherd who defends and shows care, into a wild beast that tears to pieces. The aim of such aggression is to shake Israel out of the false security drawn from the prosperity of the country, the opulence of the kingdom and the might of its armed forces. The people, in fact, are feeding on this false security and forgetting God:

> But when they had fed to the full,
> they were filled, and their heart was lifted up;
> therefore they forgot me.
> So I will be to them like a lion,
> like a leopard I will lurk beside the way.
> I will fall upon them like a bear robbed of her cubs,
> I will tear open their breast,
> and there I will devour them like a lion,
> as a wild beast would rend them (Hos 13:6-8).

42. I WILL BE TO THEM LIKE A LION (Hos 13:7)

Jasper seal of Jeroboam II with the effigy of a roaring lion, discovered at Megiddo, Israel (VIII century BC; University of Haifa).

These images used by Hosea are truly strong and contrasting! In a dramatic rôle-play, provoked by the need not to lose Israel, God, the shepherd becomes a wild beast!

A more positive aspect of the pastoral symbolism is found where Yahweh brings a 'case' against Israel and against Judah:

> I am the Lord your God from the land of Egypt;
> I will again make you dwell in tents,
> as in the days of the appointed feast.
> I spoke to the prophets;
> it was I who multiplied visions,
> and through the prophets gave parables (Hos 12:9-10).

These words of hope, arriving unexpectedly, give the impression of a glimmer of light in the darkness. In the broader context, in fact, God is making a series of accusations against Israel and Judah; and in the preceding verse we find the affirmation that Ephraim (name for the North), satisfied with its wealth, has no fear of punishment for the sins it commits. And yet, God announces a brighter future.

After reminding them of the theme of the liberation from Egypt, when he rightfully became the God of Israel, Yahweh, promises to bring back the days in the desert, when the people dwelt in tents, like bedouins who roam in search of pastures and water. The specification 'as in the days of reunion' suggests that, as well as the tents of the people, the prophet evokes also the tent in which God dwelt in the midst of his people and met with them: called, therefore, the tent of reunion, or of the meeting.

Against this background of a return to the desert, there is also described the rôle of the prophets together with that of the patriarchs:

> Jacob fled to the land of Aram,
> there Israel did service for a wife,

and for a wife he herded sheep.
By a prophet the Lord brought Israel up from Egypt,
and by a prophet he was preserved (Hos 12:12-13).

While not stating it explicitly, the text leads us to understand that the prophets carry on the rôle of the fathers (Jacob) and of the leaders of the people (Moses). The task of Jacob and of Moses is indicated by the use of a very common verb, *shamar*, 'to take care of the flock'. Used in this sense, the verb *shamar* adds richness to the pastoral terminology (see Ps 121).

In conclusion, by means of pastoral symbolism, Hosea succeeds in presenting two aspects of the divine action, seemingly opposite, but in reality complementary. God shepherds his people and cares for them through the leaders he gives them in the various phases of their history; but he can also transform himself into a wild beast that slaughters the flock. The object is the same: his infinite mercy.

AMOS

**Thus will the
Israelites be spared**

The same theme of mercy is present in a passage of the prophet Amos, the first to associate the theme of the remnant with the pastoral metaphor. Amos himself is a shepherd and cultivator of sycamores. Born in Tekoa, a little village in Judea, located about 17km south of Jerusalem, he was sent to prophesy in the kingdom of the north, therefore in the same environment as Hosea.

This man, snatched against his will from the life of a shepherd to become a prophet, feels (as Jeremiah did later) powerless to hold out against the word of the Lord: "The lion has roared; who will not fear? The Lord God has spoken; who can but prophesy?" (Amos 3:8). The prophecy of Amos is also thundering and razor-sharp: he employs no half measures nor accommodating tones.

Israel, corrupted by prosperity and egoism, advances resolutely on the road to perdition. The 'day of the Lord' will not indeed be a day of salvation, as the people expected, but rather a day of judgement: "As if a man fled from a lion, and a bear met him; or went into the house and leaned with his hand against the wall, and a serpent bit him" (Amos 5:19).

On account of the widespread injustice (plundering, violence, lack of righteousness), and notwithstanding all this, of the indifference of the rulers, God announces the arrival of an enemy who will plunder Israel (Amos 3:10-11). From the text we are given to understand that God gives his consent to this destruction. But suddenly he recalls his rôle as shepherd and intervenes to save a remnant, though it be in wretched and almost desperate conditions, shreds of prey snatched from the jaws of a ferocious beast:

Thus says the Lord:
As the shepherd rescues from the mouth of the lion two legs,
or a piece of an ear, so shall the people of Israel
who dwell in Samaria be rescued,
with the corner of a couch and part of a bed (Amos 3:12).

Reflected in these words is an experience in the life of the shepherd that Amos has probably met with (see 5:19). To snatch a prey from the mouth of the lion or the bear is a prowess which David boasts about (1 Sam 17:34). God accomplishes this feat to guarantee, despite all, a remnant of his people.

In the same social context, therefore, different uses of the pastoral symbolism are observed. In Hosea, it is introduced to denounce the situation of prosperity and infidelity ("in their pastures they have satisfied themselves and forgotten me"). God reacts violently to the situation rather than risk losing his people – he changes from a shepherd to a wild beast). In Amos, the image appears after this great chastisement, to indicate an action which is both punitive and salvific. The concept of the remnant suggests decimation, but also the survival of a minority, which by the power of God, will have a better future. To find the promise of salvation in the message of this caustic prophet, one has to look right at the end:

43. SO SHALL THE PEOPLE OF ISRAEL BE RESCUED (Amos 3:12)

Phoenician ivory plaque with gold inlays, lapis-lazuli and cornel from the palace of King Assurnasirpal II (883-859 BC) at Nimrud, Iraq (now conserved at the Iraq Museum of Baghdad).

"In that day I will raise up the booth of David
that is fallen and repair its breaches,
and raise up its ruins,
and rebuild it as in the days of old;
that they may possess the remnant of Edom and all the nations
who are called by my name,"
says the Lord who does this (Amos 9:11-12).

The booth (*sukkah*) is originally the place where livestock was gathered (Gen 33:17) and during the 40 years of nomadic living in the desert it was also the habitation for Israel. In this sense of the term, it is equivalent to a tent. In the memory of nomadic life, the people are obliged to live in huts for seven days (feast of *Sukkot*: Lev 23:42-43). In his oracle to David, Yahweh promised to construct him and his descendants a house (2 Sam 7:11); and in the biblical tradition, the house of David designates the dynasty of Judah (see, for example, 1 Kings 12:19, 20, 26). Now Amos announces the destruction that will reduce the house to a booth.

The expression is, therefore, evocative on many levels. Speaking of the hut of David, instead of the house, the prophet refers to the decimation of the ruling classes. However, there is more:

44. I WILL REBUILD IT AS IN THE ANCIENT TIMES
(Amos 9:11)

Sentry and archer on the walls of a battlemented fortress. Detail from a bronze quiver of Assyrian inspiration, discovered in Luristan, western Iran (VIII century BC; Jerusalem, Borowski Collection).

the Lord also assures a new stability after the restoration, which is connected to the ideal of nomadic and precarious lifestyle incarnate in the pastoral life. In this sense, the idea of the hut refers to the monarchy, and contrasts with the palaces of ivory against which Amos had railed. That which the Lord will raise up will not be a palace but a *sukkah*, a tent, which does not humiliate the poor man, accentuating social differences. It will not become a false security, like the dwellings in Samaria, contested by the prophet because they helped the people to forget Yahweh. On the contrary, the tent evokes that precariousness which has enabled Israel to place their trust in God, because when they dwelt in tents they lacked nothing: the Lord had procured all that was necessary.

In erecting the tent of David again, Yahweh does not simply put together again the situation he demolishes, but he restores it to the freshness of the nomadic origins of the people, and in a Davidic model. And finally, it will be the idea of the tent which will distinguish the dominion of Israel over the nations, as is suggested by the text: "I will raise up the booth/tent of David... that they may possess... all the nations". Not, therefore, the superpower of a dynasty but a humble ruling class (booth/tent) that trusts in the Lord.

MICAH

He opens the breach and walks at their head

The 'remnant' spoken of by the prophet Amos is an idea also present in Micah, but with a much more positive connotation, synonymous with 'a mighty nation' (Mic 4:7).

Micah, originating like Amos from Judah (from Morosheth-Gath, a village south west of Jerusalem), carries out his ministry going backwards and forwards between the plain of Judah, the *Shefela* – his birthplace – and the court of Jerusalem. He is an 'elder' (*zaqen*) of the people, a representative of the small landowners before the central government. As such, he defends the rights of family properties against the abuses of power exercised by the court, which tended to expropriate the landowners to reward high officials and to meet the costs of the army.

The reign of Hezekiah, during which Micah pronounced the greater part of his oracles, is characterized, in fact, by an intense military preparation, in the light of the Assyrian attack against Jerusalem that occurred in 701 BC The miraculous liberation of the city gave rise to the idea of a messianic liberation: the gathering of the dispersed and the glory of the people under the rule of a Davidic king.

During the siege of Jerusalem there was also the intervention of the prophet Isaiah who counselled and sustained Hezekiah.

The closeness of contact between the two prophets explains some similarities between them. In the account of the siege (related in parallel style in the Second Book of Kings and in Isaiah) we find a positive conception of the 'remnant' of Israel, similar to that in Micah:

> And the surviving remnant of the house of Judah shall again take root downward, and bear fruit upward; for out of Jerusalem shall go forth a remnant, and out of Mount Zion a band of survivors. The zeal of the Lord of hosts will accomplish this (Is 37:31-32; 2 Kings 19:30-31).

Micah turns to the pastoral image to illustrate the hope of Israel for the gathering of the nation, but then he too – like Hosea and Amos – bluntly alters his tone, introducing the military image:

> I will surely gather all of you, O Jacob, I will gather the remnant of Israel; I will set them together like sheep in a fold, like a flock in its pasture, a noisy multitude of men.
> He who opens the breach will go up before them; they will break through and pass the gate, going out by it. Their king will pass on before them, the Lord at their head (Mic 2:12-13).

The combination of the two images – shepherd and warrior-king – is functional in a thematic sequence that foresees the articulation of three interventions or salvific moments: the gathering of the people, their growth, and their ultimate victory over their enemies. In the succeeding passage a theme is announced which will be taken up and amplified by Ezekiel 34: the tender care of God towards the weak and infirm of his flock. The divine shepherd is both nurse and therapist:

> In that day, says the Lord, I will assemble the lame and gather those who have been driven away, and those whom I have afflicted; and the lame I will make the remnant; and those who were cast off, a strong nation; and the Lord will reign over them in Mount Zion from this time forth and for evermore (Mic 4:6-7).

The nation has become mighty and victorious thanks to the leadership and care of its shepherd-king, and now feels strong and aggressive – no longer sheep, but lions, capable of attacking and dominating other nations:

> And the remnant of Jacob shall be among the nations, in the midst of many peoples, like a lion among the beasts of the forest, like a young lion among the flocks of sheep, which, when it goes

45. HE WHO OPENS THE BREACH WILL GO UP BEFORE THEM (Mic 2:13)

Kudurru, a boundary stone in black limestone from Susa, Iraq (XIII-X century BC; London, British Museum). The stone depicts a king or an armed god protecting the property.

through, treads down and tears in pieces, and there is none to deliver

Your hand shall be lifted up over your adversaries, and all your enemies shall be cut off (Mic 5:8-9).

Micah's vision of the future does not end here. It foresees, beyond the aggression and conquest, a pilgrimage of peoples, once hostile and now converted to Yahweh, proceeding towards Zion to be instructed in the law of the Lord. The text concludes with an idyllic pastoral vision: the people will not learn the art of war any more. Each will enjoy his small piece of land and his house, the family inheritance, without having anything to fear, in perfect harmony with everyone and the environment:

It shall come to pass in the latter days
that the mountain of the house of the Lord
shall be established as the highest of the mountains,
and shall be raised up above the hills;
and peoples shall flow to it,
and many nations shall come, and say:
"Come, let us go up to the mountain of the Lord,
to the house of the God of Jacob;
that he may teach us his ways
and we may walk in his paths."
For out of Zion shall go forth the law,
and the word of the Lord from Jerusalem.
He shall judge between many peoples,
and shall decide for strong nations afar off;
and they shall beat their swords into ploughshares,
and their spears into pruning hooks;
nation shall not lift up sword against nation,
neither shall they learn war any more;
but they shall sit every man under his vine and under his fig tree,
and none shall make them afraid;
for the mouth of the Lord of hosts has spoken (Mic 4:1-4; text almost identical in Is 2:2-5).

In this serene and harmonious vision of the relations among peoples, Micah frames the figure of the messianic king, the new David: he, too, is born in Bethlehem; he, too, is a shepherd and the king of his people. Under his reign the remnant of Jacob will no longer be a ferocious beast, but a beneficent dew:

And you, O tower of the flock,
hill of the daughter of Zion,
to you shall it come,

the former dominion shall come,
the kingdom of the daughter of Jerusalem (Mic 4:8).

But you, O Bethlehem Ephrathah,
who are little to be among the clans of Judah,
from you shall come forth for me
one who is to be ruler in Israel,
whose origin is from of old, from ancient days.
Therefore he shall give them up until the time
when she who is in travail has brought forth;
then the rest of his brethren shall return to the people of Israel.
And he shall stand and feed his flock in the strength of the Lord,
in the majesty of the name of the Lord his God.
And they shall dwell secure,
for now he shall be great to the ends of the earth.
And this shall be peace...
Then the remnant of Jacob shall be in the midst of many peoples
like dew from the Lord,
like showers upon the grass,
which tarry not for men nor wait for the sons
    of men (Micah 5:2-4, 7).

46. AND YOU, TOWER OF THE FLOCK (Mic 4:8)

Babylonian column on the triumphal road of King Nebuchadnezzar II (605-562 BC) at Babylon, Iraq.

There is no escaping the strength of the images, set in contrast one to another without subtleties or logical connection, in a rapid alternation of black and white. They are perspectives that follow closely upon one another, open to the future that God is preparing for his people, under the pastoral leadership of the messiah-king. The ideal, eschatological vision does not cancel the intermediate historical reality. This exists under the sign of violence, the domination of the strong over the weak. But the ideal incentive goes beyond history and proposes a completely new situation created by God.

The fact that the flock of God is not only gathered together and multiplies, but is even transformed into a lion that subjects the neighbouring peoples – from decimation the remnant passes to domination – is not seen in any negative light by the prophet. It is consistent with the reversal of situations and of rôles that characterize the historic journey, and that God transforms in a progressive plan of salvation.

On the other hand, this striking language, made up of strong images which are by no means conventional, testifies to biblical realism. The metaphor of the shepherd and flock, far from being interpreted in the cloying tones of a certain style of devotional homiletics, holds together the idea of justice, guaranteeing the right to life of the flock, with the idea of extreme grace and benevolence.

JEREMIAH
A nation betrayed by its shepherds

Jeremiah's reflection is decisive for the understanding of the theme we are developing. The image of the shepherd continues to depict the attitude of God, but with the addition of a certain polemical note (already alluded to in Micah chapter 3) against the political and religious leaders, the so-called shepherds of the nation. This is sufficient to indicate a change in the political and social situation: we are, in fact, on the verge of the deportation to Babylon.

It is the most tormented period in the life of the people of Israel, and particularly in the personal life of Jeremiah. More than any other prophet he was involved in the tragedy of Jerusalem, under siege twice within 10 years: first for three months (598), 16 months the second time (587), and finally razed to the ground. Jeremiah had foretold the event and warned the leaders:

> But if you will not listen,
> my soul will weep in secret for your pride;
> my eyes will weep bitterly and run down with tears,
> because the Lord's flock has been taken captive (Jer 13:17).

The leaders of Israel had the task of administering the pastoral care of God, above all towards the poor and the weak. But they failed. They abused their power. They concerned themselves with personal gain, to the extent of being responsible themselves for the ruin of the flock. Hence the invectives of the prophet.

The betrayal of the covenant had reached such proportions that the judgement-punishment descended upon the whole nation:

> My people have been lost sheep;
> their shepherds have led them astray,
> turning them away on the mountains;
> from mountain to hill they have gone,
> they have forgotten their fold.
> All who found them have devoured them,
> and their enemies have said, "We are not guilty,
> for they have sinned against the Lord, their true habitation,
> the Lord, the hope of their fathers" (Jer 50:6-7).

But against the background of political and spiritual catastrophe, provoked by the wickedness and irresponsibility of the human shepherd, the great hope stands out: God does not abandon his people.

As a good shepherd, he will devote himself to the abandoned sheep: he will lead them back home; he will restore their

47. MY SOUL WILL CRY IN SECRET (Jer 13:17)

Canaanite statuette in granite (2000 BC; London, British Museum).

106

security and nurture them. And he will entrust them to shepherds 'after his own heart'.

In Jeremiah the pastoral metaphor conveys three fundamental themes:

    a. judgement against the wicked shepherds;
    b. the direct pastoral intervention of the Lord;
    c. the promise of shepherds after Yahweh's own heart, and, on the horizon, the messianic hope.

These three aspects are all present in Jeremiah 23:1-8 (a text that is taken up and developed in Ezekiel 34), while in other passages of Jeremiah the scheme is only partially present.

The judgement against the wicked shepherds

The intervention of God is expressed primarily as a critical judgement, as a stand openly taken against the ones most accountable for the dispersion of the people. There is all the intensity of divine jealousy in the invective of Jeremiah 23:1:

> "Woe to the shepherds who destroy and scatter the sheep of my pasture!" says the Lord.

It is not just any flock that they are destroying, but the flock of *his* pasture, the property he himself has acquired, by personal intervention (exodus and covenant). The shepherds have dared to claim possession of this flock as their own property, deriving personal profits from them and, worse still, causing their dispersion:

> "You have scattered my flock, and have driven them away, and you have not attended to them" (Jer 23:2a).

Consequently, the first salvific intervention of God will be that of restoring justice, calling to judgement the leaders responsible:

> "Behold, I will attend to you for your evil doings", says the Lord (Jer 23:2b).

In the original Hebrew, there is an ironic play on words: the same verb (*paqad*, 'to visit') is used both for the flock and the shepherds, but with opposite connotations: the shepherds have not 'visited' the flock (in a positive sense) and therefore Yahweh 'visits' them (negative sense).

48. I WILL ATTEND TO YOU FOR YOUR EVIL DOINGS (Jer 23:2)

Two Canaanite wrestlers. Limestone relief from the royal palace of Gozan, Syria (X-IX century BC; Berlin, Staatliche Museum).

Direct intervention of the divine shepherd

The Lord promises to bring about a new exodus (from Babylon) in a sovereign and gracious manner: he himself will go after the sheep, he will search for them, he will gather them together and bring them back to their own land; no one shall be at his side. No prior condition is requested: it is the mark of Yahweh to accomplish everything unconditionally.

The figure of the scattered sheep is most appropriate to convey the utter impossibility of their 'returning home by themselves'. As opposed to other animals, sheep are incapable of finding their way back unaided. They need someone to go after them and bring them back to the sheepfold; otherwise, once astray, they will be lost completely. Therefore, the Lord says:

> Then I will gather the remnant of my flock out of all the countries where I have driven them, and I will bring them back to their fold, and they shall be fruitful and multiply (Jer 23:3).

> Hear the word of the Lord, O nations,
> and declare it in the coastlands afar off;
> say, "He who scattered Israel will gather him,
> and will keep him as a shepherd keeps his flock".
> For the Lord has ransomed Jacob,
> and has redeemed him from hands too strong for him
>   (Jer 31:10-11).

Shepherds after Yahweh's own heart

While in the first exodus the dominating figure is that of Moses ('I am sending you'; 'set my people free'), in this and other analogous oracles related to the second exodus there is no human mediation. Only when the liberation is accomplished does God entrust the flock to human intermediaries, who will be worthy of their calling:

> I will set shepherds over them who will care for them, and they shall fear no more, nor be dismayed, neither shall any be missing, says the Lord (Jer 23:4).
> And I will give you shepherds after my own heart, who will feed you with knowledge and understanding (Jer 3:15).

On this foundation will be raised up the promised Davidic descendant, described as a branch: a life that sprouts in fragility and is almost unhoped for. He will rule wisely and establish justice and righteousness in the land:

Behold, the days are coming, says the Lord, when I will raise up for David a righteous Branch, and he shall reign as king and deal wisely, and shall execute justice and righteousness in the land. In his days Judah will be saved, and Israel will dwell securely. And this is the name by which he will be called, "The Lord is our righteousness" (Jer 23:5-6).

In this passage various elements are found which will be taken up and expanded upon by Ezekiel. Above all, there is the connection of the new king with David and with the prerogatives of wisdom and justice which characterized his house. In other words, the reigns of David and of Solomon are seen as the ideal model of royalty. Another element exists in the fact that both Judah and Israel (the two traditional parts of the Davidic kingdom) will be able to live in security, no longer in fear of their enemies.

The oracle ends underlining the magnitude of what God is about to accomplish: the new work of bringing back and of saving is such that it will substitute the traditional references to the wonders of the exodus from Egypt. Accustomed as they are to recalling the ancient prodigies of Yahweh, the people are confronted with a far greater event. Consequently, the oaths that seal social obligations will in future be made using this new formula of faith: "As the Lord lives who brought up and led the descendants of the house of Israel out of the north country and out of all the countries where he had driven them" (Jer 23:8).

EZEKIEL
The shepherd-God and the new David

Ezekiel bore witness to the downfall of Jerusalem, to the dissolution of the state and to the bitterness of the exile. He is a 'son of man' in the hand of the Lord who calls him, who guides him in every step he has to take and inspires his every word. The Lord is the only protagonist of history. In the face of the destruction of the traditional structures of the kingdom, religion and society in general, God proposes a new reality which he will create with scarcely any human participation. He will act sovereignly by 'his holy name'.

The vast and mighty programme of restoration described in Ezekiel chapters 40-48 (new temple, new form of worship, new city, new land) is preceded by a series of preparations in which Yahweh, makes a clean sweep of the old order, and yet, prepares for the new. In this sense, one can interpret the oracle against Edom, which represents all the enemies of Israel (Ezek 35:1-15), the triumph over the armies of Gog (Ezek 38-39), and the promise of renewal and resurrection for the people (Ezek 36-37).

In this context of preparation, there is extensive use of the pastoral image in chapter 34 and an echo in chapter 37. Taking up the themes and the provocations of Jeremiah, Ezekiel creates a highly evocative context of dramatic proportions. The scene could be constructed as a tribunal. The trial is in progress: on one side stand the accused (the wicked shepherds), on the other the dumb witnesses of their injustices (the sheep), and Yahweh in the centre as accuser and judge.

Woe to the shepherds of Israel

The first act of this sacred dramatization is concerned with the sentence against the false shepherds (Ezek 34:2-10). It contains the list of the various counts of indictment, the judgement and the sentence. The sin of the last leaders of Israel, which in the Second Book of Kings is globally defined as "they did what was evil in the sight of the Lord" (2 Kings 23:32,37), is invested with social connotations in Ezekiel 34.

The first indictment – "You eat the fat, you clothe yourselves with the wool, you slaughter the fatlings..." (Ezek 34:3) – consists of the rights of the shepherd, the reason why a flock is raised. However, at this point the image goes to another level. For the accused, that right does not exist because the only proprietor of Israel is the Lord.

The other accusations are all negative ones, a sequence of omissions:

The weak you have not strengthened,
the sick you have not healed,
the crippled you have not bound up,
the strayed you have not brought back,
the lost you have not sought... (Ezek 34:4).

The shepherds, therefore, have seriously neglected their duties: they have not shown the least bit of concern for the weak and infirm, for all those who needed their care, thereby rendering themselves blameworthy for the dispersion of the flock:

So they were scattered, because there was no shepherd;
and they became food for all the wild beasts.
My sheep were scattered,
they wandered over all the mountains and on every high hill;
my sheep were scattered over all the face of the earth,
with none to search or seek for them (Ezek 34:5-6).

Notice, therefore, the sentence that the Lord God pronounces against the shepherds:

Thus says the Lord God, "Behold, I am against the shepherds; and I will require my sheep at their hand, and put a stop to their feeding the sheep; no longer shall the shepherds feed themselves. I will rescue my sheep from their mouths, that they may not be food for them" (Ezek 34:8, 10).

This harsh sentence finds its parallel in Exodus 3:8 where Yahweh declares that he has come down to snatch (*natsal*) his people from the hand of the Pharaoh. The dramatic aspect, which the reader cannot fail to grasp, is reinforced by the fact that in like manner the shepherds are placed on the same level as the Pharaoh. But there is one difference: in the Pharaoh's case, there was open knowledge of his hostility as the declared enemy, whereas the shepherds, whilst embodying the rôle of leaders and protectors, are themselves devouring the flock!

Here are the two texts in concordance:

49. I WILL RESCUE MY SHEEP FROM THEIR MOUTH (Ezek 34:10)

Canaanite bass-relief in basalt from Gozan, Syria (XI-X century BC; Berlin, National Museum).

Exodus 3:8	Ezekiel 34:10.13
And I have come down to *deliver* them *from the hand* of the Egyptians, and to bring them up out of that land to a good and broad land.	And I will *deliver* my sheep *from their mouth,* that they may not be food for them. And I will bring them into their own land; and I will feed them on the mountains of Israel.

In search of the lost sheep

The second act of our drama relates Yahweh's intervention to accomplish exactly what the shepherds had failed to do. The voices are identical but the order is inverted:

I will seek the lost, and I will bring back the strayed, and I will bind up the crippled, and I will strengthen the weak, and the fat and the strong I will watch over; I will feed them in justice (Ezek 34:16).

Here a new exodus is unfolding which foresees the return of all the sheep 'from all the places where they have been scattered' and their being led back to 'their own land':

And I will bring them out from the peoples, and gather them from the countries, and will bring them into their own land; and I

111

50. I MYSELF WILL SHEPHERD
THEM (Ezek 34:15)

Semitic woman with baby. Wood statuette from Useri funeral outfit at Beni Hasan, Egypt (XII dynasty. 1990-1785 BC; Edinburgh, Royal Scottish Museum).

will feed them on the mountains of Israel, by the fountains, and in all the inhabited places of the country.

I will feed them with good pasture, and upon the mountain heights of Israel shall be their pasture; there they shall lie down in good grazing land, and on fat pasture they shall feed on the mountains of Israel.

I myself will be the shepherd of my sheep, and I will make them lie down, says the Lord God (Ezek 34:13-15).

At first sight it is surprising to find, following this salvific intervention, a second 'judgement', directed this time against the flock (Ezek 34:17-22). But we have now reached the third act of the drama.

I will judge between sheep and sheep

The scene takes us back again to the hall of judgement. One can imagine that, having heard the sentence against the shepherds, the sheep would have breathed a sigh of relief: it is not their fault! But, in truth, the end of the second act has already led us to expect a judgement on the sheep, since God says, "the fat and the strong I will destroy" (Ezek 34:16). However, the versions often adopt the reading of the Septuagint: "the fat and the strong I will watch over" (RSV).

Now the judge turns towards the sheep and points an accusing finger at them. Even in the midst of the flock (people) there are instances of arrogance and abuse of power: domination of the strong over the weak, and disdain for others:

> Is it not enough for you to feed on the good pasture, that you must tread down with your feet the rest of your pasture; and to drink of clear water, that you must foul the rest with your feet? And must my sheep eat what you have trodden with your feet, and drink what you have fouled with your feet? (Ezek 34:18-19)

These things may seen insignificant, but that is not the case. It is not enough to remove the ruling class in order to bring about salvation! Here Ezekiel recalls a theme dear to him, that of personal responsibility (cf. Ezekiel 18) and of the consequent judgement:

> Behold, I, I myself will judge between the fat sheep and the lean sheep. Because you push with side and shoulder, and thrust at all the weak with your horns, till you have scattered them abroad, I will save my flock, they shall no longer be a prey; and I will judge between sheep and sheep (Ezek 34:20-22).

A second David

The fourth act of the drama brings the solution. The sentence is pronounced on both parties in the trial, and the solution is given unexpectedly by a new character in the scene. A mysterious figure is evoked, one who will appear in the future yet who belongs to the past: a second David. He will be a shepherd like David before him, a prince (*nasi'*) like an ancient leader of the people, as if to restore royalty to its original dimensions.

The shepherd and the flock

The shepherd of flesh and blood, if he has the flock he does not have the pasture, if he has the pasture, he does not know which pasture is good. But the Holy One, blessed be he, is not like this, he has the flock, that is Israel: *And you are my sheep, the sheep of my pasture* (Ezek 34:31). He has the pasture: *The earth is the Lord's and the fulness thereof* (Ps 24:1). He knows how to pasture: *I myself will be the shepherd of my sheep* (Ezek 34:15). And he knows which pasture is good, as it is written: *I will feed them with good pasture* (Ezek 34:14).

(*Yalqut Shim'oni* II, 900b).

"What more am I to do for them?" asked God. "Let my servant David feed them," as is said *And I will set up one shepherd over them, and he shall feed them, even my servant David* (Ezek 34:23). David answered, "Thou art the deliverer; be thou also the shepherd; *Save thy people and bless thine inheritance; feed them also, and carry them*

for ever (Ps 28:9)."
(*Midrash* Ps 29:1)

Just as sheep, even when they injure trees, are not held responsible by their owners, so also even though Israel sin, God treats them like sheep. Lest you should think that just as sheep receive no reward, so it is also with Israel; since they are called sheep, the verse assures us, *And ye my sheep, the sheep of my pasture, are men* (Ezek 34:31) – you are sheep when it comes to punishment, but men when it comes to receiving reward.

In case you say: Just as sheep are intended for slaughter, so is Israel, he, therefore, calls them *holy sheep* (ibid. 36:38). He who touches anything holy becomes liable to punishment; the same is true of him who afflicts Israel, for it says, *Israel is the Lord's hallowed portion, his first fruits of the increase; all that devour him shall be held guilty, evil shall come upon them* (Jer 2:3).

(Ex R. 24:3)

The shepherd of Israel is linked to his flock by bonds of tenderness and goodness. He knows how to pasture it.

This new David is above all the 'servant' ('ebed) of God, in full agreement with him about how he is to shepherd the flock. The title of servant certainly conveys a sense of subordination, but it is not this aspect which is foremost in the relationship. Paramount is the sense of belonging to the Lord and the trust that the servant places in him. Moses is the servant of God *par excellence* (the title is attributed to him 40 times in the Bible), but king David was also distinguished traditionally with the title of *'abdi*, 'my servant' (2 Sam 3:18; 7:8; 1 Kings 11:13, 32; etc.).

The future David fulfils the ideal plan. God is the Lord of the flock, and he is the good shepherd who in no way usurps the divine lordship over the sheep. The text suggests a complete integration between the work of this servant and that of God. It is said, in fact, that David will be the shepherd, but the description that follows right to the end of the chapter is again attributed to God, so much so that it becomes impossible to separate the workings of one from those of the other.

This perfect understanding between the Lord of the sheep and the shepherd-David finds its expression in blessings and prosperity, in a covenant of peace:

> And I, the Lord, will be their God,
> and my servant David shall be prince among them;
> I, the Lord, have spoken.
> I will make with them a covenant of peace
> and banish wild beasts from the land,
> so that they may dwell securely in the wilderness
> and sleep in the woods...
> And you are my sheep, the sheep of my pasture,
> and I am your God, says the Lord God (Ezek 34:24-25, 31).

Ezekiel speaks again of the new David at the conclusion of chapter 37, after illustrating the resurrection of Israel with the powerful imagery of the dry bones. Israel will not only rise up and return to its own land, but it will also return reunified, overcoming the traditional rivalries between the two parts, Judah and Israel:

> And one king shall be king over them all;
> and they shall be no longer two nations,
> and no longer divided into two kingdoms...
> My servant David shall be king over them;
> and they shall all have one shepherd.
> They shall dwell in the land where your fathers dwelt
> that I gave to my servant Jacob;
> they and their children and their children's children
> shall dwell there for ever;

51. I WILL BREAK THE BARS OF THEIR YOKE (Ezek 34:27)

Statuette in painted wood representing a Semitic prisoner (I millennium BC; Israel, University of Haifa).

and David my servant shall be their prince for ever.
I will make a covenant of peace with them;
it shall be an everlasting covenant with them;
and I will bless them and multiply them,
and will set my sanctuary in the midst of them for evermore...
And I will be their God, and they shall be my people
   (Ezek 37:22-27).

In this text, there is a title that did not appear in Ezekiel 34, although the context there conveyed the same sense: *melek*, king, which is the usual title for the ruler. *Melek* appears here (in a central position) between the titles of servant and shepherd. The combination of these three titles (servant – king – shepherd) creates a note of tension. From a semantic point of view, the two terms servant and king are exact opposites. Even taking into account the religious significance that the word 'servant' presents here, there remains a sense of incongruity in this combination, implying that the contrast is intentional. It would seem that by the very arrangement of the titles; the author would like to correct the despotic idea of royalty (which Israel had experienced) and replace it with a conception more consonant with the pastoral function of the Davidic kingship. Hence, the use of the terms in this way has an effect analogous to that found in Ezekiel 34 with the use of *nasi'*, 'prince'.

So, the messianic David will be a servant of God, totally subject to him; a king, or rather, deputy of the sovereignty of God; and a shepherd dedicated to the well-being of the people.

SECOND ISAIAH
The joy of the return

In the lyrical passage that opens the so-called Book of Consolation (Is 40:1: "Comfort, my people"), the return to Jerusalem has the pace and solemnity of a procession. The one who is returning is God himself. With a mighty voice his coming is announced by the herald, or, better still, the messenger of Zion (in Hebrew, *'mebasseret'* 'evangelizer' is feminine), who swiftly runs ahead and climbs to the top of a high mountain to announce the good news:

Behold, the Lord God comes with might,
and his arm rules for him;
behold, his reward is with him,
and his recompense before him (Is 40:10).

The content of this beautiful message (the Greek text of the Septuagint introduces here for the first time the verb *euangelizomai*, 'to evangelize') is quite different from the mili-

52. SPEAK TENDERLY TO
JERUSALEM (Is 40:2)

*Limestone statuette from
Babylon, Iraq (III millennium
BC; London, British Museum).*

tary or political meaning, which the term evangelize, good news, usually conveyed in the contemporary Hellenistic environment.

The herald does not shout, "Our men are arriving", but rather, "Behold, the Lord God comes". It is he who, is really returning to Jerusalem and is bringing Israel with him. The good news of the messenger of Zion is addressed first of all to the holy city and then to the cities of Judah, with one wave following the other:

Speak tenderly to Jerusalem,
and cry to her that her warfare is ended... (Is 40:2).

Get you up to a high mountain,
O Zion, herald of good tidings;
lift up your voice with strength,
O Jerusalem, herald of good tidings,
lift it up, fear not;
say to the cities of Judah, "Behold your God!" (Is 40:9).

Like a counterpoint, within this double proclamation, an unknown voice announces two opposing realities: on the one hand, the sovereign passage of the Lord that transforms the shape of the desert; on the other, the fragility of man (including the mighty who held Israel in bondage) who is like grass or a flower before the scorching breath of God:

A voice cries,
"In the wilderness prepare the way of the Lord,
make straight in the desert a highway for our God.
Every valley shall be lifted up,
and every mountain and hill be made low..." (Is 40:3-4).

A voice says, "Cry!" And I said, "What shall I cry?"
All flesh is grass, and all its beauty is like the flower of the field.
The grass withers, the flower fades,
when the breath of the Lord blows upon it...(Is 40:6-7).

Seldom in Scripture do we find such a profound and penetrating conception of the sovereignty of God and of the weakness of humanity as in the prophet Isaiah, whether it be in the authentic writings of the prophet himself from the eighth century BC, or in the subsequent redactions of his disciples (to which belongs the text quoted above).

As in the times of the exodus, Yahweh advances with signs of power, his arm outstretched and victorious, guaranteeing the deliverance of Israel. He conquers their enemies and takes possession of their wealth, placing it before him as a trophy of war.

Yet, this is not all, for the voice cries out to the heart of Jerusalem that the God who comes in might is the same God who walks meekly as shepherd, attentive to the various needs of his flock and to the pace of the individual sheep:

> He will feed his flock like a shepherd,
> he will gather the lambs in his arms,
> he will carry them in his bosom,
> and gently lead those that are with young (Is 40:11).

The image is both poetic and profoundly theological, for it expresses the twofold aspect of the coming of God: Yahweh comes with might to overthrow their enemies; he comes bending low to lift Israel onto his shoulders. In other words, the God of the exodus (from Egypt and Babylon) is a God who triumphs, but he is also a shepherd who bends down to raise up his sheep, with an attitude of tenderness and mercy.

In this regard, the passage from Isaiah 40 could be read together with Jeremiah 31:

> Behold, I will bring them from the north country,
> and gather them from the farthest parts of the earth,
> among them the blind and the lame,
> the woman with child and her who is in travail, together;
> a great company, they shall return here.
> With weeping they shall come,
> and with consolations I will lead them back,
> I will make them walk by brooks of water,
> in a straight path in which they shall not stumble;
> for I am a father to Israel, and Ephraim is my firstborn.
> "Hear the word of the Lord, O nations,
> and declare it in the coastlands afar off;
> say, 'He who scattered Israel will gather him,
> and will keep him as a shepherd keeps his flock'" (Jer 31:8-10).

God promises to lead the remnant of Israel back from distant lands, and the emphasis is placed upon those who walk with difficulty: the blind, the lame, pregnant women and those giving birth (in Isaiah 40, the mother ewes). The people the Lord leads back will proceed at the pace of the one who is most handicapped. There is to be no hurrying ahead, but all are to go at the same pace as the last. This clearly illustrates the mighty work of salvation and the fact that Yahweh does not forget anyone. He accomplishes a total restoration of the people, beginning with individuals, the weak, and the marginalized.

In Isaiah 40:11, the salvation of the both the individual and the people as a whole is wonderfully expressed. God gathers together the flock, the community, with his arm. But the community that results from his powerful action is more than just a random grouping of people. In it, every individual has their own special place and very particular attention is given to the weak (the mother ewes and the newborn lambs). All will experience divine comfort and protection on the homeward journey. Even the blind are able to proceed quickly because they will not meet with any obstacles in their path.

So, for the ex-prisoners, a picture of peace and consolation is conveyed.

They will have nourishment and rest since their leader is the good shepherd, the God who has compassion:

Like a shepherd
he carries them on his breast

What is the difference between one who is engaged in [study of] Scripture and *Mishnah* [and one who is not]? By what parable may the question be answered? By the parable of a mortal king who had sons and servants whom he loved with utter devotion.

He sent them to [study] Scripture and *Mishnah*, and to learn a useful occupation. Then he waited and yearned for their return, saying, "When will they return that I may see them?" But when he saw that they were not coming, he got up and went to them and found them reading [Scripture], reciting [*Mishnah*], and engaged in a useful activity. Thereupon he seated them on his lap, took them into his arms, held them close, and kissed them. Some [were gathered] against his shoulders, some in his arms, some in front of him, some behind him, as is said, *As a shepherd that feedeth his flock, that gathereth the lambs in his arm, and carrieth them in his bosom, and gently leadeth those that give suck* (Is 40:11).

You might suppose that since God humbles himself in acting like a shepherd, he is to be considered as ordinary as any other person. But does not the very next verse say of him that *he hath measured the waters in the hollow of his hand, and meted out heaven with a span*, etc. (Is 40:12)? You must therefore admit that He acts like a shepherd only because his compassion for the world is abundant.

(*Tanna Debe Eliyyahu*, 194-195)

Gaining leverage on Isaiah 40:11, the Midrash *links the study of the Scripture and of the tradition* (Mishnah) *with the image of the father and the shepherd. It describes God in terms of a human figure ("of flesh and blood"), thus illustrating his sentiments towards Israel.*

They shall feed along the ways,
on all bare heights shall be their pasture;
they shall not hunger or thirst,
neither scorching wind nor sun shall smite them,
for he who has pity on them will lead them,
and by springs of water will guide them
    (Is 49:9-10, text quoted in Rev 7:16-17).

The prophet Zephaniah, a contemporary of Jeremiah, also sings of the joy of being tended by the divine shepherd. He is a gentle, but sometimes terrifying, prophet (see the proclamation of 'the day of the Lord' in Zeph 1:15-16). Yet, he manages to achieve a good balance between the threats and the promises, accentuating the positive elements with a view to a change in behaviour. He also had a significant influence on the religious reform carried out by King Josiah (622 BC).

With reference to our theme, Zephaniah links the pastoral symbolism to the idea of a 'remnant' of Israel, which is humble and poor, freed both from the shame of sins committed in the past and from the risk of committing any more in the future:

On that day you shall not be put to shame
because of the deeds by which you have rebelled against me;
for then I will remove from your midst your proudly
    exultant ones,
and you shall no longer be haughty in my holy mountain.
For I will leave in the midst of you a people humble and lowly.

ZEPHANIAH
The poor will graze in my pastures

53. I WILL LEAVE IN THE MIDST OF YOU A HUMBLE PEOPLE (Zeph 3:12)

Frescoes from the Egyptian tomb of Menna (reign of Tutmosis IV; 1412-1402 BC) at Thebes.

They shall seek refuge in the name of the Lord,
    those who are left in Israel;
they shall do no wrong and utter no lies,
nor shall there be found in their mouth a deceitful tongue.
For they shall pasture and lie down,
    and none shall make them afraid (Zeph 3:11-13).

This is the fulfilment of what the prophet Isaiah had predicted in the years preceding the invasion by Sennacherib, in an oracle addressed to the Philistines, Israel's traditional enemy. For them there is no hope, their remnant will be eliminated, but the poor of Israel will find pastures in the nurture of the Lord:

Rejoice not, O Philistia, all of you,
that the rod which smote you is broken,
for from the serpent's root will come forth an adder,
and its fruit will be a flying serpent.
And the firstborn of the poor will feed,
and the needy lie down in safety;
but I will kill your root with famine,
and your remnant I will slay (Is 14:29-30).

The short book of Zephaniah closes with a promise of salvation. Although at times it does not appear in the modern translations, the concluding lines echo the pastoral imagery as expressed in the language of Micah, Ezekiel and also Second Isaiah. The terms shepherd and flock are not explicitly mentioned, but the feminine adjectives refer to sheep, as does the verb 'to gather'. Moreover, Zephaniah underlines the special care that the Lord reserves for the weaker members. Just like Micah, he affirms that, in spite of their present condition, once reunited, the people will become famous and an object of praise among all the peoples of the earth:

Behold, at that time I will deal with all your oppressors.
And I will save the lame (sheep) and gather the outcast,
and I will change their shame into praise and renown
    in all the earth.
At that time I will bring you home,
at the time when I gather you together;
yea, I will make you renowned and praised among
    all the peoples of the earth,
when I restore your fortunes before your eyes, says the Lord
    (Zeph 3:19-20).

The last prophet to make extensive use of the shepherd metaphor is Zechariah. The writing that bears his name has a similar history to that of Isaiah: part of it dates back to the prophet himself, whilst part of it is the work of the school of his disciples. The whole work is the result of a successive re-elaboration. Nevertheless, in both parts, echoes and themes of the more ancient prophets are recognizable.

The departure from Babylon, celebrated in Second Isaiah as a solemn return, as almost a procession following the shepherd-King, in Zechariah becomes a plea to escape addressed to those who are still loitering by the rivers of Babylon (Zech 2:6-7).

He urges the reconstruction of the temple. "Let your hands be strong", the prophet exhorts them, "the day that the foundation of the house of the Lord of hosts was laid, that the temple might be built" (Zech 8:9). The Jews and other peoples of the earth shall come together to seek the Lord there:

Thus says the Lord of hosts:

Peoples shall yet come, even the inhabitants of many cities; the inhabitants of one city shall go to another, saying, "Let us go at once to entreat the favour of the Lord, and to seek the Lord of hosts; I am going."
Many peoples and strong nations shall come to seek the Lord of hosts in Jerusalem, and to entreat the favour of the Lord.
Thus says the Lord of hosts:
In those days ten men from the nations of every tongue shall take hold of the robe of a Jew, saying, "Let us go with you, for we have heard that God is with you" (Zech 8:20-23).

To this same Jerusalem, a centre of pilgrimage for many peoples and a house of prayer for all, will come the long-awaited Messiah-King, humbly riding a colt. He will do away with weapons of war and will herald lasting peace:

Rejoice greatly, O daughter of Zion!
Shout aloud, O daughter of Jerusalem!
Lo, your king comes to you;
triumphant and victorious is he,
humble and riding on an ass, on a colt the foal of an ass.
I will cut off the chariot from Ephraim
and the war horse from Jerusalem;
and the battle bow shall be cut off,
and he shall command peace to the nations... (Zech 9:9-10)

The salvation of Israel is etched on the horizon, depicted in two images – sheep and jewels – seemingly contrasting, or at

ZECHARIAH

The shepherd who is killed and the new covenant

121

least unrelated, but both highlighting the preciousness of the people:

On that day the Lord their God
will save them for they are the flock of his people;
for like the jewels of a crown
they shall shine on his land (Zech 9:16).

The parable of the two shepherds

Like other prophets before him, Zechariah receives the command to announce the word of the Lord by means of very peculiar behaviour. He has to pasture sheep doomed to slaughter, in order to be a symbol of the shepherd Yahweh.

The conditions for those sheep are desperate. The buyers butcher them with impunity: the right is theirs, as they paid for the goods. The sellers are glad they have sold them, "Blessed be the Lord, I have become rich". As for the shepherds to whom they were entrusted, they do not care at all (cf Zech 11:4-5).

So the prophet continues to pasture the sheep on behalf of the merchants. He procures two staffs: the first he names 'Grace', the second 'Union': names clearly alluding to the behaviour of God towards Israel and his plan of salvation.

At the end of a month of pastoral activity (that is to say, a brief period), Zechariah has already achieved notable success, eliminating three shepherds unworthy of the name. But a disconcerting factor takes over: despite his use of Grace and Union, the sheep grow weary of him, they can no longer bear his presence. Against his will he is obliged to abandon them (like Moses, who after killing the Egyptian is forced to flee because of his brothers):

54. HE WILL ANNOUNCE PEACE
(Zech 9:10)

Painting from an Egyptian tomb from Thebes (1500 BC; London, British Museum).

In one month I destroyed the three shepherds.

But I became impatient with them, and they also detested me. So I said, "I will not be your shepherd.

What is to die, let it die; what is to be destroyed, let it be destroyed; and let those that are left devour the flesh of one another."

And I took my staff Grace, and I broke it, annulling the covenant which I had made with all the peoples.

So it was annulled on that day, and the traffickers in the sheep, who were watching me, knew that it was the word of the Lord.

Then I said to them, "If it seems right to you, give me my wages; but if not, keep them." And they weighed out as my wages thirty shekels of silver.

Then the Lord said to me, "Cast it into the treasury" – the lordly price at which I was paid off by them. So I took the thirty shekels of silver and cast them into the treasury in the house of the Lord. Then I broke my second staff Union, annulling the brotherhood between Judah and Israel (Zech 11:8-14).

The reader who is familiar with the gospel narratives will undoubtedly have noticed the various allusions in this passage. Those 30 pieces of silver are the price agreed upon for Judas Iscariot to hand over Jesus (Mt 26:15 and parallel texts); they, too, will be thrown into the temple treasury, and Matthew relates the fulfilment of the Scripture (Mt 27:3-10).

In actual fact, 30 shekels is a paltry price (the price of a slave: Ex 21:32); given as wages to the prophet they introduce a note of mockery and contempt, even more so as the price for the Just One! In the Hebrew text the expression already refers to the Lord; it reads: the 30 shekels with which *I have been valued* by them, and not: with which *you have been valued*, as is to be expected. So there is to be understood here an identification of God with the person and the work of the prophet.

But it is above all the behaviour of the sheep (people) that sounds ungrateful and scornful towards the prophet, the only one who showed concern for them. It will be no different for Jesus. He who walked among the people doing good, will be abandoned by them and handed over to be killed.

Leaving behind the sheep for slaughter, Zechariah receives a new command from the Lord. He must impersonate a stupid and foolish shepherd, who could not care less about the sheep, and yet – it goes without saying – the sheep follow him:

For lo, I am raising up in the land a shepherd who does not care for
    the perishing,
or seek the wandering, or heal the maimed, or nourish the sound,
but devours the flesh of the fat ones, tearing off even their hoofs
    (Zech 11:16).

This account has a sour taste to it. Where is the joyful promise of shepherds after the heart of Yahweh? History would appear to repeat itself without notable variations. In the space of about 200 years, this text recalls the accusations of Ezekiel against the shepherds responsible for the ruin of Israel. Here too, even more than in Ezekiel, the responsibility of the sheep is beyond discussion. "I will not be your shepherd. What is to die, let it die." How thankless and discouraging is the task of leading a people who stubbornly refused to understand the benevolence of the Lord! But this is not Zechariah's last word.

Awake, O sword, and strike my shepherd!

Chapter 13 begins with this announcement, "There shall be a fountain opened for the house of David and the inhabitants of Jerusalem to cleanse them from sin and uncleanness" (Zech 13:1). The end is decreed for the idols as well as for the institution of prophets, who were guilty of having served them rather than the Lord, and of pronouncing lies in his name. Therefore there will be a purification and a profound revitalization of the inhabitants of Jerusalem. But not without cost. At the end of chapter 12 and immediately after this announcement, a mysterious person is spoken of, one who will be pierced (seemingly by the same inhabitants of Jerusalem), whom they will nevertheless gaze upon filled with the spirit of grace and consolation. They will mourn for him as for only child:

> And I will pour out on the house of David and the inhabitants of Jerusalem a spirit of compassion and supplication, so that, when they look on him whom they have pierced, they shall mourn for him, as one mourns for an only child, and weep bitterly over him, as one weeps over a firstborn (Zech 12:10).

There is a disturbing element in this extraordinary text coming from the mouth of Yahweh. The original text says: "they will look on *me* whom they have pierced", and then, "they shall mourn for *him*". The reading proposed by RSV – "they will look on *him* whom they have pierced" – is an amendment of the difficult original 'me' used in the Hebrew. But the original text can be understood without corrections if one maintains that the one who is pierced is actually the same Yahweh who has been rejected. This explains the abrupt transition from the first to the third person.

Once again, in Zechariah 13:7, there is a person who is killed. Yahweh calls him "my shepherd, the man who stands next to me" (*geber 'amiti*) and yet he hands him over to the sword, a symbol of suffering and death. There follows the

55. AWAKE SWORD (Zech 13:7)

Stele of Sihan. Hittite bass-relief discovered in the excavations between Dibon and Sihan to the east of the Dead Sea, with the effigy of a king (Paris, Louvre Museum).

scattering of the flock, but not completely. For God stretches forth his hand to help the weak, and 'one third' of the people – a remnant – passes victoriously through the final test, symbolized by fire.

Then the days of the new covenant foreseen by Jeremiah (31:31-34) will be fulfilled; the Lord will acknowledge that third as 'his people' and they will call him their God:

> Awake, O sword, against my shepherd,
> against the man who stands next to me, says the Lord of hosts.
> Strike the shepherd, that the sheep may be scattered;
> I will turn my hand against the little ones.
> In the whole land, says the Lord,
> two thirds shall be cut off and perish, and one third shall be
>   left alive.
> And I will put this third into the fire,
> and refine them as one refines silver,
> and test them as gold is tested.
> They will call on my name, and I will answer them.
> I will say, "They are my people";
> and they will say, "The Lord is my God" (Zech 13:7-9).

56. THEY WILL CALL ON MY NAME (Zech 13:9)

Musician in clay from Ugarit, Syria (XIII century BC; Museum of Damascus).

Jesus applied this oracle of Zechariah to himself while on the way towards his passion and death:

> And when they had sung a hymn, they went out to the Mount of Olives.
> And Jesus said to them, "You will all fall away; for it is written, 'I will strike the shepherd, and the sheep will be scattered'. But after I am raised up, I will go before you to Galilee" (Mk 14:26-28 = Mt 26:30-32).

As in Zechariah, so too from the mouth of Jesus the killing of the shepherd and the consequent scattering of the flock are not the last word. A new beginning is foreseen, made possible by that victorious death: the appointment in Galilee, where the risen shepherd will re-establish his flock.

We have been able to establish how rich and stimulating the metaphor of the shepherd is in the Prophets . It gives continuity to a fundamental idea, tried and tested in the story of the exodus: the personal involvement of the Lord in the liberation and leading of his people, an involvement so gracious and bountiful that the 40 years in the desert are remembered as a time of special care and providence.

The stimulus of prophecy

On the other hand, the prophets notably enrich the significance of the pastoral metaphor by means of evocations, echoes and new uses. This is mainly seen in Hosea. Then from the mouth of Amos the image is interwoven with the idea of the remnant, presenting an almost desperate act of salvation: shreds of prey snatched from the jaws of the lion; yet at the same time heralding a reconstruction of the monarchy on humble and temporary foundations: the hut of David.

Micah underlines that the pastoral care of Yahweh is preferential: it is concerned with the weak and the scattered, the injured sheep and the ones who have gone astray. This aspect will never be forgotten by subsequent prophets; it is dear to Jeremiah, but also to the Second Isaiah and Zechariah. They will confirm that it is by paying attention to the least, by strengthening the feet of the those who walk with difficulty that it is possible to advance together with confidence towards Jerusalem and construct a better future.

The sin of the shepherds of Israel, denounced by the prophets, lies precisely in their failure to attend to the needs of the little ones and the weak so as to devote themselves solely to personal gain. For Ezekiel, placing personal interests before those of the flock constitutes a perversion of pastoral ministry. Moreover, this can also result from neglect, from not performing one's own duties: what you should have done you have not done!

What should the shepherds of Israel have done, what was their specific task? This can be easily worked out from the denunciation of their omissions. They ought to have strengthened the weak, cared for the infirm, bound up the dislocated, led back those who had strayed, searched for the lost, and devoted themselves with goodness and meekness to the well-being of all.

The vehement 'woes' of Jeremiah and Ezekiel really do unmask the ever recurring temptations of history: the thirst for power; the forming of impersonal relationships with others for reasons of self-interest, such as economic gain, cultural advantage, or any mercenary motive; or worse still, the opposite extreme of not relating at all because others are seen as of no interest or value.

In the history of the tradition, it is observed that the invectives of Jeremiah and Ezekiel have been taken up by other prophets, for example, Zechariah, but rarely by any rabbis or other Jewish commentators. On the other hand, they have been quoted by the Fathers of the Church not merely as polemic against the wicked shepherds of Israel (as some phrases would readily suggest), but rather to alert leaders of Christian communities to the attitudes and behaviour denounced by the prophets (see Discourse of St Augustine on Ezekiel 34).

Prophecy never fails to shake up and stimulate. The fact that pastoral responsibility calls to account not only the leaders, but the entire community (see the judgement between sheep and sheep) is another important aspect brought to light by Ezekiel. In contrast to the *Midrash* which interprets the image of the sheep in the sense of a limited responsibility which would spare the people from their deserved punishment (see Ex R. 24:3; similar text for Num 23:2), the prophet confronts each one with personal responsibility. It is not enough to lay the blame on those who govern. Everyone is responsible for everyone else, so that none can live only for themselves, neglecting the needs and the rights of others (Ezek 34:18-21).

But above all, in the prophetic writings, the image of the shepherd carries a message of hope, bound to the strong and passionate love of the Lord. The affection he nurses for his people is so strong that nothing succeeds in diminishing it. If he punishes, it is for correction; if he distances himself, he then goes in search of them; if he assails his flock like a wild beast, it is because he cannot resign himself to losing them. Yahweh himself is the true archetype of the good shepherd (see Ezek 34:11-16). His providence surrounds those faithful to him and goes before them on their journey. The poor and the humble who trust in him will be able to rest in the pastures of the Lord and quench their thirst at springs of water, as Isaiah and Zephaniah promise in their prophetic songs.

So then, how shall we describe the divine shepherd? Perhaps Isaiah has the best definition: "He who has pity on them" (Is 49:10).

Song and Wisdom

As well as prophecy, Israel has experienced the beauty of song, praise and poetry. Often, the same prophets have expressed their message in lyrical form, according to the poetic canons of Hebrew literature, realizing moments of extraordinary beauty and emotional intensity, as in Isaiah or Jeremiah.

One particular area in which poetry expresses all its force is that of worship. In proclaiming the praise of Yahweh, Israel recalls the marvellous works he accomplished when he freed them from the yoke of Egypt and led them for 40 years, until he brought them into the land promised to their fathers.

We have already noted the strength of this singing to Yahweh when speaking of Miriam, the prophetess who on the shores of the Red Sea intones the chorus and leads the dancers. While it celebrates an event already accomplished, the song unites the present to the past. In fact, those who sing of a past liberation, also sing with hope in their hearts, or besieged by the present, they find refuge in this memory and sustain their hope.

It is precisely in this capacity of unifying time and life that song and poetry exert their most fascinating appeal. Like other nations, Israel succumbed quickly to that influence. This is particularly confirmed in the psalms (*tehillim*), the heart of biblical spirituality, where lamentation, anger and sometimes imprecations are interwoven with cries for help, and with blessing of the works and the holy name of Yahweh. The whole of life, with its ever-changing states of soul and emotions, the present situation, but equally the past and the future, even the moment of death with its mysterious beyond, are assumed into song and unified in praise. In this way, the moment of worship becomes the privileged sphere in which the history of salvation is celebrated, and which renders possible the singular experience of this unification of time and life.

How is the pastoral symbol present in this context and what message does it transmit? There are at least 12 psalms that refer to Yahweh as a shepherd, or to Israel as the flock of the Lord. Among these, Psalm 23, the song to the Good Shepherd, stands out for its beauty.

57. I WILL SING TO THE LORD
(Ex 15:1)

Egyptian parietal painting from Thebes (1500 BC; London, British Museum).

128

Moreover, the Song of Songs also presents a shepherd and a shepherdess in a pastoral love scene. The magnificent text of Ecclesiasticus represents the universal mercy of God in the figure of the shepherd, and the conclusion of Ecclesiastes affirms that

> The sayings of the wise are like goads, and like nails firmly fixed are the collected sayings which are given by one Shepherd (Eccles 12:11).

Poetry and wisdom, therefore, together re-read the past, revisit the ancient accounts of salvation and translate their meaning into the new context of life, drawing from them inspiration for today and tomorrow.

The expression that re-echoes, almost unchanged, in Psalms 74, 79, 95 and 100 could appear to be a stereotyped formula:

> Then we thy people, the flock of thy pasture (Ps 79:13).

PSALMS

Consciousness of the covenant

Yet this phrase certainly lacks the coldness of the stereotype. Rather, it could be seen as the crystallization of a profound consciousness that touched the very identity of Israel: the awareness of an altogether singular belonging to Yahweh, as his property (*segullah*) out of all the peoples of the earth (see Ex 19:5).

In the psalms mentioned above, the terms 'people' (*'am*) and 'flock' (*tso'n*) are perfectly interchangeable, to the point that side by side with "your people, the flock of your pasture" (Ps 79:13), we find "people of his pasture and flock of his hand" (Ps 95:7). Again, the expression "flock of his hand" is explained by Ps 100:3: "It is he that made us, and we are his; we are his people, and the sheep of his pasture". Flock and people whom God himself has created with his strong arm, taking possession of them from their slavery in Egypt and caring for them with his providence.

Consequently, the image of the flock, far from expressing a disparaging connotation, or at least one lacking in esteem (as it would imply today), in biblical language positively denotes the idea of a people. There are two reasons. Firstly, because it is rooted in the lived experience of ancient Israel when the flock was the only property, and thereby the most important possession, constituting the economic value and wealth of a nomadic group of people. Secondly, between flock and shepherd there is seen to exist a special relationship of closeness and intimacy.

When the people of Israel sing "We, your people and the flock of your pasture", they are expressing the strong sense of belonging that comes from having been chosen as the personal property of the Lord, and at the same time the affective dimension of such a bonding. Even while tilling the soil or engaging in commerce, the people continues to see itself as 'the flock of the Lord' and 'people of his pasture'. This language is seen, on the one hand, to express the complete confidence of the praying community, and on the other, the boldness to question God and recall him to his duties towards Israel.

These two aspects of trust and audacity emerge particularly in Psalms 74 and 79, attributed to Asaph. They are both psalms of lamentation for the looting of the temple and for the desolation afflicting the chosen people:

O God, the heathen have come into thy inheritance;
they have defiled thy holy temple;
they have laid Jerusalem in ruins.
They have given the bodies of thy servants
to the birds of the air for food,
the flesh of thy saints to the beasts of the earth.
They have poured out their blood like water
round about Jerusalem,
and there was none to bury them.
We have become a taunt to our neighbours,
mocked and derided by those round about us (Ps 79:1-4).

O God, why dost thou cast us off for ever?
Why does thy anger smoke against the sheep of thy pasture?
Remember thy congregation,
which thou hast gotten of old (Ps 74:1-2).

The great humiliation because of the profanation of the temple and the destruction of Jerusalem provokes the interrogation of Yahweh. The one who prays is not satisfied with traditional, or at any rate discounted, answers. If the sin of the fathers was such as to merit exile, the very honour of the Lord could not tolerate the further mocking of his people:

How long, O Lord
Wilt thou be angry for ever?...
Let thy compassion come speedily to meet us,
for we are brought very low...
Why should the nations say,
"Where is their God?"
Let the groans of the prisoners come before thee;
according to thy great power
preserve those doomed to die! (Ps 79:5, 8, 10-11).

58. HOW LONG, O LORD?
(Ps 79:5)

Praying figure. Elamite statuette in bronze from Susa, Iraq (XII century BC; Paris, Louvre Museum).

With surprising boldness the psalmist plays on the pride of the Lord: a fine impression his name is making among the nations! If it is true that he liberated his people from Egypt, how is it that he does not intervene now? Where is his power, his mighty protection? Intervene, Lord, because you have compromised yourself and the honour of your name! We are the flock of your pasture and you cannot permit that they tear us apart with impunity!

> Return sevenfold into the bosom of our neighbours
> the taunts with which they have taunted thee, O Lord!
> Then we thy people, the flock of thy pasture,
> will give thanks to thee for ever;
> from generation to generation
> we will recount thy praise (Ps 79:12-13).

We again find this same formula of covenant in Psalm 95, which was sung for the feast of shelters (*sukkot*), when Israel celebrated the memory of the 40 years lived whilst wandering through the desert. The faithful went up in procession towards the ruin of the temple where the most significant hut (*sukkah*) had been made ready. During the ascent they were invited to acclaim Yahweh as mighty God, 'great king above all gods', creator of the sea and of the earth, of the depths (abysses) and the heights (mountain peaks), and above all, of humanity and of Israel his people:

> O come, let us worship and bow down,
> let us kneel before the Lord, our Maker!
> For he is our God,
> and we are the people of his pasture,
> and the sheep of his hand (Ps 95:6-7).

In this psalm the pastoral image is linked with the memory of wandering in the desert, marked by the provident care of the Lord, but also with the stubborn resistance of the people. There follows the invitation to listen 'today' to his voice, and not repeat the sin of their fathers, sorely putting the patience of God to the test:

> O that today you would hearken to his voice!
> Harden not your hearts, as at Meribah,
> as on the day at Massah in the wilderness,
> when your fathers tested me,
> and put me to the proof,
> though they had seen my work (Ps 95:8-9).

59. LET US KNEEL BEFORE THE LORD (Ps 95:6)

The Amorite King Ham-murabi praying. Statue in gold and bronze from Larsa, Iraq (Paris, Louvre Museum).

Proclaiming themselves to be 'people of his pasture', Israel recalls the exodus and all that the 40 years in the desert signified in terms of pastoral care on the part of the Lord, learning from the memory of it the lessons vital to their present condition. It was their way of saying, "If you claim to be the people of his pasture, you should trust in him, listen to his voice and feed on his word. And do not, like your fathers did, proclaim the word and lordship of Yahweh and then in your actions and decisions continue to be preoccupied about yourselves, saying, 'What shall we eat, what shall we drink?' (see Mt 7:31), as if God had not already made you touch and handle his providence."

This invitation to acknowledge the lordship of Yahweh and, consequently, the fact that Israel is his creature and special possession, lies at the heart of Psalm 100, the last of the series (Psalms 93-100) dedicated to the divine kingship:

> Know that the Lord is God!
> It is he that made us, and we are his;
> we are his people, and the sheep of his pasture (Ps 100:3).

Remembrance of the past

Why does the psalmist turn to the image of the flock in order to play on the sentiment of God? The reason is because this image is linked to the memory of a glorious past: to the time of the exodus when God personally went out 'at the head of his people', like a shepherd walking ahead of his sheep:

> O God, when thou didst go forth before thy people,
> when thou didst march through the wilderness,
> the earth quaked, the heavens poured down rain,
> at the presence of God;
> yon Sinai quaked at the presence of God, the God of Israel.
> Rain in abundance, O God, thou didst shed abroad;
> thou didst restore thy heritage as it languished;
> thy flock found a dwelling in it;
> in thy goodness, O God, thou didst provide for the needy
>   (Ps 68:7-10).

60. WE, YOUR PEOPLE
    (Ps 79:13)

Singers count time with the clapping of hands. Detail from a limestone relief from the palace of the Assyrian King Assurbanipal at Nineveh, Iraq (VII century BC; London, British Museum).

It would almost seem that while singing of the wandering in the desert, Israel is again able to feel itself in contact with the hand of God who, as a good shepherd, provides water and nourishment and revives their confidence, "Blessed be the Lord, who daily bears us up; God is our salvation" (Ps 68:19).

In Psalms 77 and 78, both attributed to Asaph, the memory of the past is evoked in the difficulty of the present condition (as in Psalms 74 and 79). The psalmist is overwhelmed with anguish for the affliction of his people, and God seems absent. Disturbed by God's silence he prolongs his vigils, meditating on the past and asking himself:

I consider the days of old,
I remember the years long ago.
I commune with my heart in the night;
I meditate and search my spirit:
"Will the Lord spurn for ever,
and never again be favourable?
Has his steadfast love for ever ceased?
Are his promises at an end for all time?
Has God forgotten to be gracious?
Has he in anger shut up his compassion?" (Ps 77:5-9).

"Certainly not!" should be the reply to this series of questions; but the conclusion of the psalmist is something different:

And I say, "It is my grief
that the right hand of the Most High has changed." (Ps 77:10).

In other words, the tradition of faith attests to the everlasting mercy of the Lord (see, for example, Is 49:14-16), but the psalmist's heart is seized with doubt and crushed with grief. "The Lord is no longer the same; he has grown weary of us, he has abandoned us! How can an escape be made from this tunnel of distrust, this night of the spirit and of faith?"

The psalmist claims to have found light by reflecting on the past. But in what sense and why? What important discovery does he make that bears on the present situation? The key to this reading lies hidden in the conclusion of the psalm. On the one hand, past history bears witness to a unique and grandiose manifestation of divine guidance, "Thy way was through the sea, thy path through the great waters" (Ps 77:20). On the other hand, even then that presence remained mysterious and imperceptible. No one discerned the footprints of the shepherd who walked ahead and opened up the way. It was through the mediation of human 'shepherds' that Israel experienced his leading:

Yet thy footprints were unseen.
Thou didst lead thy people like a flock
by the hand of Moses and Aaron (Ps 77:19-20).

The meaning becomes clear. God at present seems far away, wrapped in silence. The question is voiced, "Where are you?" In order to find an answer, the past is revisited, that is, the time, according to the fathers, in which God was present and acted in person. There could be the temptation of reading the past in direct contrast to the present, as if it were a depository of the mythical golden age, of a divine presence almost tangible and permanent. But our psalm does not present such a reading of the past. Even when passing over the waters, throwing them into confusion, certainly in a manner which was most tangible, even then God remained hidden.

From his meditation on the past, the psalmist derives the necessity to look 'beyond', or rather to continue to believe that the one who guides history is truly the good shepherd, even if he does so by the hands of men who are not equal to Moses and Aaron.

In Psalm 78, the departure from Egypt is described in a manner that recalls the seasonal migration of livestock. God freed his people from the confines of Egypt to lead them to new pastures, as the shepherd does at the beginning of Spring:

> Then he led forth his people like sheep,
> and guided them in the wilderness like a flock.
> He led them in safety, so that they were not afraid;
> but the sea overwhelmed their enemies.
> And he brought them to his holy land,
> to the mountain which his right hand had won (Ps 78:52-54).

However, even here, as in Psalm 95, the years spent in the desert under the guidance of Yahweh the Shepherd evoke the so-called 'temptations' of the fathers:

> Yet they sinned still more against him,
> rebelling against the Most High in the desert.
> They tested God in their heart
> by demanding the food they craved.
> They spoke against God, saying,
> "Can God spread a table in the wilderness?
> He smote the rock so that water gushed out
> and streams overflowed.
> Can he also give bread,
> or provide meat for his people?" (Ps 78:17-20).

It is easy to prepare a table in proximity to shops filled with all kinds of foodstuffs. But, if food and drink run out in the desert, it is the beginning of the end. A people who are prey to hunger can understandably give in to murmuring. The sacred author, however, calls their reactions 'temptations', because the people had already experienced the mighty hand of the Lord and should have trusted in him. Hence, there is a blasphemous tone in asking if God is able to prepare a table for them in the desert. In actual fact, the psalm continues: "when the Lord heard, he was full of wrath... because they had no faith in God, and did not trust his saving power" (Ps 78:21-22). Contrary to their doubts, he showed himself to be a true shepherd, capable of laying a table even in the desert (see Ps 23:5).

The past is also revisited to invoke salvation in the present in another psalm attributed to Asaph, Psalm 80. In the psalms already examined, Yahweh is said to be a shepherd only implicitly, indirectly, insofar as Israel is spoken of as his flock and the people of his pasture. But here the identification resounds explicitly and solemnly in the title 'Shepherd of Israel', which our psalmist finds particularly effective to solicit the divine intervention:

Give ear, O Shepherd of Israel,
thou who leadest Joseph like a flock!
Thou who art enthroned upon the cherubim, shine forth
before Ephraim and Benjamin and Manasseh!
Stir up thy might, and come to save us! (Ps 80:1-2).

Within the psalm, a refrain that recurs three times:

Restore us, O God; let thy face shine, that we may be saved!
(Ps 80:3,7,19).

This refrain, by means of an interval, connects two images (or two songs): that of the shepherd, which opens the psalm, and that of the vineyard, which unfolds from verse 9 up to verse 19. The interval itself consists of a sorrowful lament:

O Lord God of hosts, how long wilt thou be angry
with thy people's prayers?
Thou hast fed them with the bread of tears,
and given them tears to drink in full measure.
Thou dost make us the scorn of our neighbours;
and our enemies laugh among themselves (Ps 80:4-6).

Returning to the poem of Isaiah (5:5-7), Asaph re-reads the past history of the exodus, and also the present situation, lamenting that so much care bestowed by the Lord for the benefit of his vineyard should now come to such a miserable end. In Isaiah, it is God who laments over his vineyard (that is, his people), since, having done so much to dig and cultivate, it yields him only wild grapes in return. By contrast, here the psalmist (and definitively the vineyard) complains against God. What point is there in having worked so much for that vineyard if now "all who pass along the way pluck its fruit?" (Ps 80:13). Like the song of the shepherd, so also this song of the vineyard is destined to make an impression on the heart of God, to turn his heart in compassion to his covenant people.

The pastoral mediation of Asaph

Five of the psalms which present the pastoral symbolism are attributed to Asaph — not an insignificant percentage of a total of 12 (three are attributed to David, one to the sons of Korah, and the others are anonymous). One of their characteristics is the particular formulation of the covenant relationship, cited above, 'his people and the flock of his pasture'.

There are indications that this symbolism is bound up with the kingdom of the North. In actual fact, Psalm 80 mentions the tribes of the North, Ephraim and Manasseh, the sons of Joseph whom Jacob blessed invoking the shepherd-God (see Gen 48:15). In the blessing of the twelve tribes, Jacob also uses that title in reference to Joseph (Gen 49:24). They are, therefore, the sons of Rachel, the shepherdess, who in the North have kept alive the tradition and the spirituality of the Shepherd-God, while in the South of the country, this tradition was preserved only by the house of David, the shepherd-king.

In this context, we seek to discover the formative concern that guided Asaph in his reflection on the past. His preoccupa-

---

Shepherd of Israel, listen!

Give ear, O shepherd of Israel (Ps 80:2).

As a year of redemption brings with it the necessities of life, so a year that brings the necessities of life brings redemption with it.

And as redemption sustains us every day, so the necessities of life maintain us every day. And as redemption is miraculous, so the necessities of life are miraculous.

The image of God the shepherd may evoke the deliverance from evil or the continuous nurturing of life.

Rabbi Samuel bar Nahmani taught: The miracle of the necessities of life is greater than the miracle of redemption, for while redemption depends upon an angel, as Jacob said, *The angel who hath redeemed me from all evil* (Gen 48:16), the necessities of life come from the hand of the Holy One, blessed be he, as Jacob said, *The God who had been my shepherd all my life long unto this day* (Gen 48:15).

Hence *Give ear, O shepherd of Israel.*

(*Midrash* Ps 80:2)

tion with recounting the parables of ancient times is directed towards the young – that they might know and not forget. At the beginning of Psalm 78 he makes himself the mouthpiece for the adult generation, addressing the youth, in continuity with the custom of previous generations:

Things that we have heard and known,
that our fathers have told us,
we will not hide them from their children,
but tell to the coming generation
the glorious deeds of the Lord,
and his might,
and the wonders which he has wrought (Ps 78: 3-4).

61. WE WILL TELL THE GLORI-OUS DEEDS OF THE LORD (Ps 78:4)

Detail from an ivory plaque from Megiddo, Israel (XIII-XI century BC; Rockefeller Archaeological Museum).

This, then, is the pastoral action of Asaph! It is found in this passing on of the living memory of faith to future generations, in order that, reflecting on the days gone by and on the events lived by their fathers, they might learn the most precious lesson for their lives: to believe in God and to hope in his salvation (cf Ps 78:22).

The testimony of Asaph passes through poetry and song: such, in fact, are the psalms according to the Greek designation (*psalmoi*); that is, poems sung to the accompaniment of a psaltery, an ancient one-stringed instrument. This explains his admiration for king David whose memory gives a positive note to the final verses of the lengthy Psalm 78. In King David, the composer of psalms and gifted player of the lyre, Asaph must surely have found his model and inspiration:

He chose David his servant,
and took him from the sheepfolds;
from tending the ewes that had young
he brought him to be the shepherd of Jacob his people,
of Israel his inheritance.
With upright heart he tended them,
and guided them with skilful hand (Ps 78:70-72).

If we compare the conclusions of Psalms 77 and 78, we will notice that in both, Asaph mentions the theme of pastoral mediation. In the first case, the divine shepherd has led his people/flock by the hand of Moses and Aaron; in the second, by the wise hand of David, who was the shepherd with the undivided heart, since he loved God and his people with the same heart.

The human mediation is important to Asaph. It is through it that God concretely guides, educates and forms the generations of his children. Asaph's activity of composing and singing psalms can also be seen in the wake of these positive mediations – as a faith-education of the young through songs and poetry. In modern terms, we would speak of a faith-education through animation and pastoral liturgy.

Behold who our God is!

The affectionate and diligent guidance of the Lord, which is invoked in Psalm 80, is celebrated as a positive and quasi-miraculous experience in Psalm 48, attributed to the sons of Korah. In the background, there is probably the defeat of the Syro-Ephraimite coalition against Ahaz in 735, and the unexpected and hasty retreat of Sennacherib in 701 (see 2 Kings 18:13-19:37):

> For lo, the kings assembled,
> they came on together.
> As soon as they saw it,
> they were astounded,
> they were in panic,
> they took to flight (Ps 48:4-5).

In such a dramatic context as this, where Israel finds itself trapped between the sea and Pharaoh's warriors, Isaiah (like Moses before him) exhorts the people to believe in the intervention of the Lord (Is 7:1-9). That day the inhabitants of Jerusalem saw, just as their fathers on the shores of the Red Sea had done, a wonderful and unhoped-for salvation. The psalmist, therefore, can conclude:

> That this is God,
> our God for ever and ever.
> He will be our guide for ever (Ps 48:14).

The guidance of the divine shepherd is also invoked at the conclusion of Psalm 28:

> O save thy people, and bless thy heritage;
> be thou their shepherd, and carry them for ever (Ps 28:9).

Both Psalm 28 and Psalm 68 are attributed to David, the shepherd called by God to become king. However, it is above all in Psalm 23 that David's experience is ideally associated with the pastoral activity of God. It is worth pausing to reflect more deeply on this psalm.

Psalm 23 is one of the most exquisite jewels in Hebrew religious poetry, permeated throughout with sentiments of trust in Yahweh, who leads and nurtures his faithful in their journey through life. It is a brief psalm (only six verses long), with a fairly regular rhythm, without any dramatic moments or great emotions. It would be regarded as easily understood, and, in fact, is one of the psalms sung most frequently in liturgical celebrations; but to the eye of the expert it is not so simple or straightforward.

It is debatable whether the first and second parts are spanned by the same image, or by different symbols. If that is the case, what is the unifying theme of the poem, and in what real-life situation did it originate? There are those who place it against the background of the exodus or the Davidic traditions. Those who see it better placed in the exile and exodus from Babylon; and those who classify it among the psalms of pilgrimage to the temple.

We shall in the first place attempt to capture the poetic movement. We shall also see how the symbolism of the shepherd and of hospitality can be understood against the background of the exodus, but how it also lends itself to a continuous re-reading and is well adapted to illustrate the human journeying towards the house of the Lord.

Shepherd or host?

The psalm unfolds around two basic motifs: the motif of the shepherd, with which the poem commences and which characterizes the first movement (vv. 1-4), and that of the host (vv. 5-6). Beginning from verse 5 the psalmist speaks of a table prepared, oil poured over the head, the cup that overflows – a symbolism which fits better with the image of the host. Finally goodness and mercy will accompany the faithful towards the house of the Lord, where he hopes to dwell for the length of his days (v. 6).

Alongside these themes of the shepherd and the host, there is an interweaving of symbols and colours, a marked connection between *food* (lush pastures/cup overflowing) and *drink* (peaceful waters/cup overflowing); a subtle play of balance between stillness and movement, rest and journey.

Some see the structure of the psalm in three movements, better still, in three 'positions' of the divine presence: ahead, beside and behind. In the initial part, we find the shepherd who goes ahead and leads the way; at the centre, the "You" who walks beside the believer on his journey; and finally, the divine presence that accompanies, as if to encircle the entire person of the faithful. Thus we have the following structure:

PSALM 23

The Lord is my shepherd

62. YOU WILL PREPARE A TABLE FOR ME (Ps 23:5)

A banquet. Detail of an Assyrian relief from the palace of King Assurbanipal at Nineveh, Iraq (VII century BC; London, British Museum).

63. I SHALL NOT WANT
    (Ps 23:1)

Grape harvesting. Detail from a parietal painting from the tomb of Nakht at Thebes (c. 1425 BC; New York, Metropolitan Museum of Art).

- vv. 1-3   God walks ahead, leader;
- v. 4   You with me, at my side;
- vv. 5-6   God follows, with goodness and mercy.

The psalmist sings of the sweet presence which envelops the whole of his life and of the great peace and security it instils in him. Even if the path should lead to dark valleys, face-to-face with enemies, the goodness and the mercy of the Lord will accompany him all the days of his life.

Yahweh, my shepherd

Let us know analyse the psalm verse by verse. The theme of Yahweh as shepherd is introduced with extreme conciseness, with just two words in Hebrew: *Yhwh ro'î*, Yahweh, my shepherd. It is a declaration of faith, seemingly tranquil, but which includes a polemic note: Yahweh – and no one else –is my shepherd! The psalm, intended as praise, is already imbued with this faith and trust. The following verses prolong the echo, singing of the various manifestations of the pastoral care of Yahweh.

"I shall not want", the psalmist exclaims. It could also be translated, 'I shall not fall short, I shall not fail'. Not only in the sense of 'I want and I shall want for nothing', but also, 'I myself shall not be diminished, that is, I shall not fall into nothingness because my life is held in good hands'. It is a confession of faith based on concrete, human history, on both individual and plural experience. It does not spring from an abstract confession ('I believe in almighty God'), but from an experience of goodness: since God shows concern for me I will not fail, I shall want for nothing. This conviction transforms the manner of facing one's existence and permits the singing and praising of God in every situation.

In green pastures you make me rest

This is a scene of peace, of great tranquillity. The good shepherd seeks the best pastures for his flock. And since he *keeps watch*, the sheep can *rest* peacefully. The Hebrew verb *rabats* (translated as 'rest') indicates the posture of the sheep when they stretch out on the grass.

Is this just idyllic poetry? Where in Palestine can one find the expanse of green that the psalm would have us imagine? Isn't this scene in direct contrast to the reality of scorched and barren earth, which stretches before the pilgrim as he draws near to climbs towards Jerusalem? Where are these evergreen pastures and 'still waters'? The desert of Judah is "barren earth, parched and without water" (Ps 63:2), where the traditional author of this psalm, David, drove his father's sheep to pasture.

In reality, the land given by the Lord to Israel sees a miracle which repeats itself twice a year with the autumn and spring rains. Then, even the desert becomes green. That earth, scorched by the sun, is transformed ever so briefly into green pastures, into a flowering desert.

Something similar took place on a historical plane when the Lord led back the prisoners from Zion: it seemed to them like a dream (Ps 126:1). But it was reality, because he who had pity on them guided them and led them back to springs of water (see Is 49:9-10 and Rev 7:16-17).

He leads me to peaceful waters

The psalm continues with the theme of water. After the sheep have eaten and rested on the soft grass, the shepherd leads them to still waters, where they can drink and refresh themselves.

However, in this psalm, it is not merely a question of fresh and thirst-quenching water. The expression 'still waters', literally 'waters of rest', awakens in the reader a particular resonance with the text. For *menûhah*, 'rest', is essentially a synonym of *shalom*, 'peace', the sign of the divine benediction, and associated with the gift of the promised land (see Deut 12:9; 25:19; 28:65). Thus the waters of rest are meant to signify that general well-being which flows from the land and the enjoyment of its benefits.

He brings back my life

The benevolent care of the shepherd is invigorating. The RSV translation reads: 'he restores my soul'. But there is something more within the Hebrew expression. It speaks of *nefesh*, 'soul', as the supreme good that humanity has received from God and that finally returns to them, and uses the verb *shub* in the transitive sense of 'brings back'. Therefore, it is a particularly meaningful expression. Rightly, the *Midrash* compares it to another of similar density, referring to the Law: "It signifies that Israel said: God *will bring back my soul* through the *Torah*, as it is written: The law of the Lord is perfect, *reviving* the soul (Ps 19:7)".

Undoubtedly, by translating Psalm 23:3 'he restores my soul', a return of energies is intended. Yet, this translation obscures other meanings implicit in the original term. In fact, the 'return

64. HE REVIVES MY LIFE
(Ps 23:3)

A child receiving a drink. Detail of an Assyrian parietal relief from the palace of King Sennacherib (704-681 bc) at Nineveh, Iraq (London, British Museum).

141

of the soul' can be interpreted on three levels: on the historical, on the ethical, and on the eschatological.

On the historical level, *shub* could indicate the return from exile, a new exodus: from Babylon to Jerusalem. And since, according to the prophets, it was on account of their sins that Israel went into exile, so then the 'return' to Jerusalem should include an ethical movement, that is a return as *metanoia*, 'conversion'.

Now, the protagonist of the return, whether in the historical, moral or eschatological sense, is not Israel, but Yahweh. The psalmist does well to say, "he brings back my life". It is not I who decide to return, to choose conversion; it is God, the good shepherd, who 'brings back', who converts.

Finally, the return on an eschatological level is the rising out of *she'ol* (the kingdom of the dead), suggested by the walking through the valley of the shadow of death (v. 4), to dwell in the house of the Lord. The Shepherd will not leave our life in the grave, but will bring it back to himself. This is the reason why both Jews and Christians pray this psalm in the liturgy for the dead.

He leads me in paths of righteousness

In this context, the expression 'paths of righteousness' does not have a juridical significance, but rather a theological-salvific one. In the first place, it evokes the justice of God, that is to say, the work that he accomplished bringing the people out of Egypt and making them enter into their own land.

Our text applies the traditional terminology of justice (as it is found primarily in the prophets) to the symbolism of the sheep. Yet, sheep do not know which path is best for them, it is the shepherd who knows. Therefore, the 'paths of righteousness' spoken of in the psalm indicate the path that God prepares for his people. The best paths are not always the shortest or the straightest, but those chosen by the shepherd for the good of his flock. So also, the 40 years of wandering in the desert were certainly not the shortest route towards the promised land, but they suited God for the education of his people, and in that sense they were paths of righteousness.

Moreover, it is on account of his faithfulness – "for his name's sake" recites the psalmist – that God behaved in such a manner.

Even though I walk in a dark valley...

Not even darkness brings fear if the Shepherd is present. To express 'valley of darkness' (*tsalmawet*) the Hebrew text uses a word that contains the term 'death' (*mawet*). In a passage from Job, the same word describes the kingdom of the dead, a place of no return:

Let me... before I go whence I shall not return,
to the land of gloom and deep darkness (Job 10:21).

The original Hebrew expresses this close link between darkness and death, an association frequently made through the use of collective imagery. In every age, popular fantasy has imagined death as a monster with a huge mouth that swallowed people alive. Fear of the dark is a very common experience associated with memories of childhood. But the child who walks hand-in-hand with his 'daddy' is not afraid.

This illustrates well the experience of the psalmist. Even if the road passes through a dark valley, reminding him of death, he declares himself fearless of any evil. Why? "Because you are with me." The presence of the shepherd instils complete security: on him rests the psalmist's peace of mind for today and tomorrow.

The object on which our courage depends transcends us, and yet it is not far away. He walks beside us. His presence journeys with us and keeps watch over our steps: "He will not allow your foot to stumble, he sleeps not, your guard.... He will preserve you from all evil, he will preserve your life", proclaims Psalm 121.

An episode from the life of Jacob comes to mind, where the same expression appears as in Psalm 23:4. The patriarch receives orders to return to Bethel to construct an altar on the site where God had appeared to him when he was fleeing from Esau. In this undertaking, he involves the family and all who were with him, he invites them to purify themselves and says to them, "Let us go up to Bethel, that I may make there an altar to the God who answered me in the day of my distress and has been with me wherever I have gone" (Gen 35:3).

So our psalm celebrates the overcoming of the great fear of death through the presence of the shepherd-God. The opposite is found in Psalm 49, in which wicked men are depicted as sheep consigned to the depths, with Death in person as their shepherd:

Like sheep they are appointed for Sheol;
Death shall be their shepherd... (Ps 49:14).

65. YOUR ROD AND YOUR STAFF (Ps 23:4)

Mede servant. Limestone relief from the palace of the Assyrian King Sargon II (721-705 BC) in Khorsabad (New York, Metropolitan Museum of Art).

Your rod and your staff comfort me

How is it that the image of the staff, which we generally associate with commands and threats, is here bound up with

143

the theme of consolation? The reason is that here the rod and the staff speak of the loving presence of the shepherd. The Hebrew verb used is *naham*, the one which opens the Book of Consolation, "Comfort, comfort my people, says your God" (Is 40:1).

The staff is an important symbol for our research. The text uses two different terms to describe it: *shebet* and *mish'enet*. The *shebet* is the instrument used for striking and correcting; it designates both the rod of the shepherd and the sceptre of the king. It was not long, since to indicate the staff used for walking another term is used, *mish'enet*. By linking the two terms, the poet holds together the idea of authority, expressed by means of the rod that guides (*shebet*), and the idea of journeying together with the flock, expressed by the shepherd's crook (*mish'enet*, translated as staff for want of a better word).

The striking of the earth with the staff emphasizes the presence of the shepherd and indicates to the sheep the direction for their steps On the other hand, the shorter stick that the shepherd holds in his hand and waves in the air while passing in the midst of the flock has another function. It signals his watchful presence, ready to correct the abuses of the stronger sheep over the weak, and defends both from the attacks of wild beasts. This is why both rods comfort and console the flock.

It was actually the custom for shepherds to carry two sticks, even as the Bedouins are seen to do to this day. We recall that the prophet Zechariah named his two sticks 'Grace and 'Union'. They were symbolic names, apt to express the nature of the prophet's mission: the grace of God towards Israel and the unity of the people; but they also indicated the function of the benevolence of the shepherd who walks alongside the sheep, and as a means of keeping them united, safe from dangers without and in harmony within.

Another text which helps us to understand the function of the staff is Ezekiel 20, in which the pastoral terminology is intertwined with that of the exodus:

> I will bring you out from the peoples and gather you out of the countries where you are scattered, with a mighty hand and an outstretched arm, and with wrath poured out; and I will bring you into the wilderness of the peoples, and there I will enter into judgment with you face to face. As I entered into judgment with your fathers in the wilderness of the land of Egypt, so I will enter into judgment with you, says the Lord God. I will make you pass under the rod, and I will let you go in by number. I will purge out the rebels from among you, and those who transgress against me... (Ezek 20:34-38).

This passage highlights the punitive function of the staff: it separates the sheep who have unwittingly wandered away, from those who have deliberately rebelled against Yahweh and no longer merit the divine care. Instead, in Psalm 23, the staff is not used for striking: it indicates that the shepherd is walking with the flock and thereby is a source of joy and of consolation.

He prepares a table before me

With verse 5 of the psalm the scene changes; the shepherd becomes the host, "He prepares a table before me". It would seem that one image supplants the other, but that is not the case. Shepherd and host are in fact two images that go hand-in-hand within the context of nomadic culture. Furthermore, both images have already been presented bound together in the story of the exodus: God for Israel has been a hospitable shepherd.

The banquet spoken of is "in the presence of enemies". What does this mean? A situation of escaping danger (valley of death, enemies) which is celebrated with feasting and solemnity. The particular situation is not named, so the text remains open to various experiences of averted danger, and each can celebrate his own instance.

In the Book of Job, a charismatic youth named Elihu explains how it is through suffering that God calls humanity to change their ways. Moreover, God encourages them in this by promising them a sumptuous feast:

66. MY CUP OVERFLOWS
(Ps 23:5)

The Assyrian King Assur-nazirpal II (883-859 BC) Ivory plaque from the royal palace of Nimrud in Iraq (Baghdad, Iraq Museum).

He delivers the afflicted by their affliction,
and opens their ear by adversity.
He also allured you out of distress
into a broad place where there was no cramping,
and what was set on your table was full of fatness (Job 36:15-16).

The situation in the two texts differs: in Job the idea of correction appears, yet it is absent in the psalm. But common elements exist which disclose a constancy in the divine behaviour. As well as delivering from danger (Psalm) and by means of suffering (Job), God treats his faithful one royally, as he alone can do. In other places, too, the divine hospitality is symbolized by a sumptuous banquet, for example, the meat filled with marrow that God will prepare for all his people at the end of time (Is 25:6).

In Psalm 23, the divine largesse reflects the reality of oriental hospitality, truly bounteous: the table is richly spread, the overflowing cup and, in addition, the perfume poured on the head ("You anoint my head with oil"). The host spares no expense:

not only necessities, such as food and lodging, but even the perfume.

Ointment of the finest quality is a mark of special honour towards the guest, and it is customary in the lavish feasts. Psalm 133 uses this image to illustrate the beauty of harmony, of dwelling together:

It is like the precious oil upon the head,
running down upon the beard,
upon the beard of Aaron,
running down on the collar of his robes (Ps 133:2).

"On my head," exclaims the visibly moved author of Psalm 23.

At Bethany, Mary pours out all the costly perfume over the feet of Jesus provoking Judas to exclaim that the money from the oil would have fed many poor people (cf Jn 12:1-8). Here we see perfume as an eminent sign of grace poured out purely out of love .

In Psalm 23, the idea of munificence is reinforced by the image of the cup that overflows. One is reminded of the description of the miracle worked by Jesus in Cana of Galilee (Jn 2:1-11). Even there the Lord is not satisfied with giving the necessary quantity of wine, he gives in superabundance, six jars 'filled to the brim', an enormous quantity.

Goodness and mercy will follow me

67. GOODNESS AND MERCY SHALL FOLLOW ME (Ps 23:6)

Egyptian dancers. Parietal painting from the tomb of Nebanum at Thebes (XVI-XIV century BC; London, British Museum).

"Surely", continues the psalmist, "goodness and mercy (*tob* and *hesed*) shall follow me all the days of my life." The guest, so generously welcomed and refreshed in the tent of the shepherd, can now resume his journey.

There may still be some anxiety for the journey, perhaps the enemies are still waiting in ambush. As if to banish every fear, two messengers (or bodyguards) are present, goodness and mercy, who will accompany the psalmist all the days of his life. He can, therefore, resume his journey with courage and confidence until he reaches the final tent, the temple of the Lord.

The verb used in the last phrase of this psalm can have two meanings in Hebrew: 'and I shall dwell in the house of the Lord', or 'I shall return to the house of the Lord'. From the point of view of the consonants (vowels are not written in Hebrew) both versions are possible and we prefer to leave open the interpretation of the text.

What, then, does this closing thought say to us? It expresses the desire either to return (in pilgrimage) or to dwell forever in the temple, the house of the Lord. It is the great longing of the pilgrim, of everyone devoted to Zion: "How lovely is thy dwelling place," sings the psalmist. "Blessed are those who dwell in thy house, ever singing thy praise! For a day in thy courts is better than a thousand elsewhere" (Ps 84:1, 4, 10).

Perhaps the passage most resembling the conclusion of our psalm is the request formulated by Psalm 27:4:

One thing have I asked of the Lord,
that will I seek after;
that I may dwell in the house of the Lord
all the days of my life,
to behold the beauty of the Lord,
and to inquire in his temple.

Yes, the Lord will lead us in goodness and mercy, day after day, for the duration of our lives. And when these days come to an end, he will 'bring us back' from the depths to his house, where we shall be together for ever.

Against the background of Davidic traditions

The biblical tradition attributes the psalm to David, and not without good reason. Who better than him, the shepherd-poet and gifted player of the lyre, called from the pastures to become king, could be imagined as author of a lyric that extols the divine shepherd?

But for the critics, some elements exist that raise doubts about the tradition and point to an author after David's time. They observe, for example, that the final verse speaks of the 'house of the Lord', with obvious reference to the temple, constructed during the reign of Solomon. However, the objection is not altogether convincing, since even in the times of David there existed the 'house of the Lord', not to be confused with the temple of stone (see ark and tent). Moreover, the tradition which attributes the psalm to David should not be discarded so easily, as it can in fact be regarded as a significant key for its interpretation.

Generally, the figure of the shepherd is correlated with that of the flock, a collective image referring to a people: "We his people, the flock of his pasture", proclaims Psalm 100. But Psalm 23 speaks in the singular, "The Lord is my shepherd". Therefore, not a flock ('we'), but a single sheep ('I') is here the primary subject of the relationship with the shepherd Yahweh. What comes to mind is the parable which the prophet Nathan recounted to David, of the young sheep raised in the house of the poor man, "it used to eat of his morsel, and drink from his cup, and lie in his bosom, and it was like a daughter to him" (2 Sam 12:3).

Moreover, this one-to-one relationship recalls the way Jacob presents his God to the sons of Joseph in the land of Egypt, when he blesses them and adopts them as his own sons. He can say, "The God before whom my fathers Abraham and Isaac walked, the God who has led me all my life long to this day" (Gen 4:15).

The words of Psalm 23 then cannot but attest that the experience of Jacob has been appropriated by his sons: it has become their heritage. And yet, while expressing the faith of a people, the psalm is not presented in the plural, but in the singular. Is it possible to combine the two perspectives? If this 'my shepherd' is seen placed in the mouth of David, who is king and therefore exercises a corporate function (representative of the people), the singular naturally expresses the common reality. In this sense, the psalm interprets the faith of every child of Israel, a faith which is both a personal and common experience, "The Lord is my shepherd, there is nothing I shall want".

Against the background of the exodus

What does Psalm 23 suggest if we read it against the background of the exodus? Such an association comes naturally to the mind of the reader, even if doubt arises regarding the intention of the psalmist. But the Judaic interpreters have unanimously associated it with the tradition of the exodus. In this perspective, the psalm evokes above all the particular experience of Yahweh's pastoral care during the 40 years in the desert.

The waters of Psalm 23 recall those gushing forth from the rock in the desert (Ps 78:20; cf Ex 17); the green pastures and the miraculous manna and quails; the shepherd's staff with which Moses opened the waters of the Red Sea... The psalm could also be an allusion to the enemies that pursue Israel yet are forced to halt, astonished and impotent because God protects his people and reserves for them a splendid reception within his tent.

In the fabric of the psalm, the image of the shepherd carries the aspects of stillness, security, providence; that of the host, the extraordinary hospitality of the Lord. To the poet, it matters little that the connections are clear at a rational level; what he praises in song are the many facets of the pastoral care of the God of Israel.

In conclusion, in which lived situation could Psalm 23 have been written? We can imagine the faithful Israelites, already settled in the land of his fathers, experiencing the splendid benevolence of the Lord in his house, in the sanctuary where they have arrived in pilgrimage. There they relive the ancient events of the fathers (the wanderings of Jacob, the exodus from Egypt) and they meditate on the experience of the monarchy of David. In each of these, they perceive the sign of the pastoral care of Yahweh, which inspires confidence for the future, both as individuals and as a nation.

The Shepherd of David

He maketh me to lie down in green pastures (Ps 23:2) alludes to David when he fled from Saul. Note well where he fled: "David departed, and came into the forest of Hereth" (1 Sam 22:5). Why was it called forest of Hereth? Though it was once dry as a potsherd, the Holy One, blessed be he, covered it with blossoms out of the richness of the world-to-come, as is said, "In a dry and thirsty land, where no water is... my soul shall be satisfied as with marrow and fatness" (Ps 63:2c, 6a).

He restoreth my soul; he leadeth me in the paths of mercy for his name's sake (Ps 23:3): Here David is saying that kingship came to him not for his own merit, but *for His name's sake.*

Yea, though I walk through the valley of the shadow of death (Ps 23:4) means that David said, "In the wilderness of Ziph, *I will fear no evil*" (ibid.). Why? *Because Thou art with me* (ibid.).

Thy rod and thy staff they comfort me: the rod is chastisement, as in the phrase, "The rod of his oppressor" (Is 9:63); and staff is the Law which is as a staff unto Israel. Now lest the words *they will comfort me* might lead one to think that comfort from the written and the oral Law may be had without chastisement, therefore the word *'only'* which begins the next verse (Ps 23:6a) makes the comforting conditional. Lest one think that they comfort me only in this world, the verse goes on to say, *Goodness and mercy shall follow me all the days of my life; and I shall dwell in the house of the Lord for ever* (Ps 23:6) – goodness and mercy both in this world and in the world-to-come.

Thou preparest a table before me in the presence of mine enemies (Ps 23:5): *a table* refers to royalty; *enemies*, to Doeg and Ahithophel.

Thou hast anointed my head with oil (Ps 23:5b), with the oil of royal anointing; and *My cup runneth over* – that is, the cup of salvation, of which the Psalmist says, "I will take the cup of salvation, and call upon the name of the Lord" (Ps 116:13).

(*Midrash* Ps 23)

A reading of Psalm 23 in the light of the events of David.

You are a good shepherd

He maketh me to lie down in green pastures (Ps 23:2). Rabbi Eliezer asked Rabbi Simeon, saying to him, "As the children of Israel were going out of Egypt, did weavers' gear go out with them?" Rabbi Simeon replied, "No." "Then how did they clothe themselves those 40 years?" Rabbi Simeon replied, "With garments which the ministering angels gave them for clothing: For God said of Israel in the wilderness, *I clothed thee also with broidered work* (Ezek 16:10). How is *broidered* to be defined except, so Rabbi Simai said, 'as garment of royalty'".

"But did not their garments wear out?" – "Have you not read that Moses said to Israel in the wilderness, *Thy raiment waxed not old upon thee* (Deut 8:4)?" – "But did not the little ones among the children of Israel grow up?" – R. Simeon replied: "Go out and learn from the snail: all the while that he grows, his shell grows with him!"

"But did not the garments require washing?" – Rabbi Simeon replied, "The cloud of fire cleansed their garments, and made them shine."

R. Eliezer asked: "But were not the garments burnt?" – Rabbi Simeon replied, "Go out and learn from the amiant, which is cleansed only by fire." (...)

"But since the children of Israel did not change their garments, did they not reek with sweat?" – Rabbi Simeon replied, "The well of living waters brought up certain plants and certain spices for the children of Israel, and in these they were made to lie down, as is said *He maketh me to lie down in green pastures; he leadeth me beside refreshing waters* (Ps 23:2), and so the fragrant smell of them was carried from world's end to world's end". Solomon came and said to Israel: *The odor of thy garments is like the odour of Lebanon* (Song 4:11). (...)

When the children of Israel saw how the Holy One, blessed be he, led them and refreshed them in the wilderness, they began to offer praise to him, saying, "Thou art a good shepherd, for thou hast made us never to lack thy goodness."

(*Midrash* Ps 23:4)

The traditions of the exodus offer colourful and suggestive details, and illustrate how, beyond all their expectations, God has been the good shepherd to his faithful.

The two lovers in the Song of Songs make their first appearance under the guise of a shepherd and a shepherdess. In this collection of lyrics, the pastoral terminology blends with that of love in its stage of betrothal, where passion, pursuit, desire, encounter (the motifs follow one another in an endless circle), find their fulfilment in a subtle atmosphere which borders on both fantasy and reality.

Pastoral terminology and the terminology of love do not meet for the first time in this Song. Love, care and mercy are the unexpressed elements of the language of pastoring when it is related to God and to human leaders of the people. However, what is unique about the Song is that here the terms adhere so closely to the context that what is expressed is an almost unrivalled depth and freshness of spirit. The lovers are like children who are discovering for the very first time the horizon of life.

The horizon of life is love. Not a frivolous or care-free thing, but the love that is the divine force present in the world: that which is diffused in the blossoming of fields, of flowers, of vines, in the variety of living beings and animals. In contact with God's creation, intact as if they had just come from his hand, the young couple discover themselves, enfolded, as it were, in this great floodtide of Love, the divine reality, present in the world, that overcomes death itself. And this discovery has its origins in their lives as shepherds, in direct contact with nature.

She describes herself as very dark like the tents of the bedouins of Kedar, but beautiful like the curtains of Solomon. The sons of Kedar, descendants of Ishmael (Gen 25:13), serve to indicate the bedouin environment. The mention of Solomon (to whom the song is attributed) adds the element of royalty, which reappears from time to time in the rapport between the two young people.

She tells the chorus of the 'daughters of Jerusalem' that there is a reason for her skin being so dark: her brothers had obliged her to work in the vineyards. As if to say, let no one think ill of her. She is not a girl who loves to wander freely, out of doors, as is the custom for boys (the dark colouring is a masculine trait in the culture of the Ancient East, as is also noted in Egyptian art). Her tanned skin is due to the ruling of her brothers, who control her because she is a woman and probably because she is the youngest, still a child ("her breasts are not yet formed," Song 8:8).

But she feels mature for love. Suddenly she raises her voice to confess her desire:

Tell me, you whom my soul loves,
where you pasture your flock,

SONG OF SONGS

Tell me, my love, where you pasture your flock

68. I AM DARK AND
    BEAUTIFUL (Song 1:5)

Head of a woman in ivory from Megiddo (XIII-XII century BC; Rockefeller Archaeological Museum).

151

where you make it lie down at noon;
for why should I be like one who wanders (lit.: 'veils herself')
beside the flocks of your companions? (Song 1:7).

The young girl longs to know where she can find her lover; she does not wish to wander about and risk being regarded as a prostitute, who veils herself in the places where shepherds are found (Gen 38:14-15).

The reply she receives from the chorus of the daughters of Zion (the youth appears to be still absent) is enigmatic and is scarcely ever explained by modern commentators:

If you do not know, O fairest among women,
follow in the tracks of the flock,
and pasture your kids
beside the shepherds' tents (Song 1:8).

The chorus suggest to the young girl that she abandon her activity of taking care of the vineyard and start being a shepherdess. In this way, she can draw near to the places frequented by the shepherds without arousing suspicion, and thus finally meet with her beloved. The daughters of Jethro were also known to frequent the localities of the male shepherds, and so it is that Rachel arrives at the well where the other shepherds are already gathered.

The text seems to suggest that their common activity will permit the two young people to meet and discover together the signs of the divine vitality present in creation. Furthermore, it is evidence of feminine initiative, reversing the ancient oriental and biblical conception. In actual fact, the Song of Songs, more than any other book in the Bible, highlights the equality of the sexes, to the extent that the phrase addressed to Eve, "yet your desire shall be for your husband, and he shall rule over you" (Gen 3:16) is given the opposite meaning, "I am my beloved's, and his desire is for me" (Song 7:11).

In the Song, the various facets of the pastoral imagery are suggested by a subtle play on Hebraic roots, whether identical or similar. The poet exploits the several meanings implicit in the form of the verb *ra'ah*, which can mean 'to pasture, to eat', as well as 'to be companion, friend'. The young man is one 'who pastures (*ro'eh*) his flock among the lotus flowers' (normally translated 'lilies': 2:16; 6:3); the girl is called "my companion, my friend" (*ra'yati*: 1:9, 15 etc.); and the lotus flower could indicate either him or her (the loved one is a lotus lily among thorns, compared with her companions (Song 2:2). An analogous play on words is achieved with the term 'garden': he 'pastures his flock in the garden' (6:2); she is a 'garden' (4:12).

In this way, the basic image is amplified by a series of associations and suggestions.

The Judaic tradition re-reads some of the terms of our text allegorically, even to the extent of disregarding the connection with the original text. In the tents, it sees an allusion to the synagogue and to the house of studies, and in the shepherds, a reference to the leaders and the doctors of the law, particularly to David and Solomon. The *Targum* interprets Song 1:8 in this way:

69. MY BELOVED PASTURES
    AMONG THE LILIES
    (Song 2:16)

Detail from an Egyptian wooden casket, inlaid with ivory, from the funeral outfit of the Pharaoh Tutankamen (1333-1323 BC) at Thebes (Cairo, Egyptian Museum).

153

The Holy One, blessed be he, said to the prophet Moses, "I will go in search of them to put an end to their exile. The congregation, which is like a beautiful young girl that my soul will love, will walk in the paths of the righteous, and will order the prayer according to the rules of their *shepherds* and the *leaders* of their generations; and will teach its children, who are like young goats, to go to *the synagogue* and to *the house of study*. Because of this they will be cured for during their exile, until I send the messiah king. He will lead them to their *tents* with tenderness, that is to *the sanctuary* which David and Solomon the shepherds of Israel have built for them" (*Targum* on Song 1:8).

The *Targum* here elaborates a double interpretation of the phrase 'tents of the shepherds'. On the first level, the shepherds are identified as the spiritual guides of the people, and more precisely, with those who teach the Scriptures, the doctors of the Law; and the tents are identified with the synagogues and the houses of study. On a second level, David and Solomon are held to be the shepherds, and the tents allude to the temple.

Against this background, the *Targum* announces the coming of the Messiah. It is he who will gently lead the exiles back to the sanctuary, the dwelling place of God among humanity. But his coming is conditioned by the behaviour of the children of Israel, that is to say, by their application to the teaching and study of the *Torah*.

The targumic interpretation introduces a new element in the impact of the pastoral symbol: the figure of the shepherd as teacher and doctor, and correspondingly, of the tent as the place of the teaching and study of the Word. This didactic element is not out of place in the Song, which is rightly included in the wisdom literature. The combination shepherd-teacher is explicit in the two wisdom texts to be treated in the following section, and will have a special prominence in the New Testament.

ECCLESIASTICUS

Ben Sirach: the shepherd-teacher

Not only the language of love, but also that associated with wisdom makes use of the pastoral symbolism to convey its message. The connection love-wisdom-shepherd already actualized in the Song, reappears in a beautiful text of Ecclesiasticus, where the creative wisdom of the Lord is interpreted as universal mercy.

Ben Sirach is a teacher of wisdom who, in the context of the Hellenist crisis preceding the Maccabean revolt, intends presenting the perennial value of the ancient biblical wisdom to the young generations, above all of the middle classes, who most are exposed to seduction by pagan culture.

This contribution consists in integrating the wisdom transmitted by his predecessors with a passionate study of the Torah, which was practised mostly among the priests. In his effort to develop a new synthesis of biblical wisdom, he displays a great pedagogic sensitivity. As a sage, he extols the beauty of the universe and the goodness of the Creator who reveals himself in it; as a scholar of the Torah, he assumes the pastoral image (that was particularly bound up with the exodus) to re-formulate the experiences of the ancient sages.

In a particularly beautiful passage, the image of the shepherd, with the functions of vigilance and of affectionate care that characterize it, is employed to re-shape the figure of the true teacher and pedagogue:

Their compassion is only for their own kin,
but the Lord's compassion is for all mankind.
He corrects, disciplines and teaches,
and brings them back as a shepherd brings his flock
    (Ecclus 18:13, from the Revised English Bible)

He pastures amongst the lilies

The Lord is my shepherd; I shall not want (Ps 23:1).

These words are to be considered in the light of the verse *My beloved is mine, and I am his: he feedeth his flock among the lilies* (Song 2:16), by which is meant that the congregation of Israel said to the Holy One, blessed be he: As he is God to me, so am I a people to him.

As he is God to me, having said: *I am the Lord thy God* (Ex 20:2), So am I his people to him, he having said: *Attend unto me, O my people* (Is 51:4).

As he is father to me, having said: *I am a father to Israel* (Jer 31:9), so am I son to him, he having said: *Israel is my son* (Ex 4:22).

As he is shepherd to me, Asaph having said: *Give ear, O shepherd of Israel* (Ps 80:2), So am I sheep to him, he having said: *Ye my sheep, the sheep of my pasture* (Ezek 34:31).

As he is brother to me, Solomon having said: *Oh that thou were as my brother* (Song 8:1), so am I sister to him, he having said: *Open to me, my sister, my love* (Song 5:2).

As I said to him: *The Lord is my shepherd, I shall not want,* he said to me: *Thy navel is like a round goblet, wherein no mingled wine is wanting* (Song 7:2).

(*Midrash* Ps 23:1)

Psalm 23 is read in the light of the Song of Songs. The flock is the bride in whom the divine shepherd finds his delight.

The mercy of the Lord towards every creature is expressed in four basic dimensions, epitomized in the rôle of the shepherd. The image functions here purely as an archetype inasmuch as it moves on an educational level, and presumably in a civic environment. And yet, that archetype is of the utmost importance, since it portrays the profound consciousness that Israel has of itself and of God in pastoral terms. In other words, Israel's self-understanding is that of a nomadic people even while living in sedentary fashion. However, it is indulging in nostalgia for the past and dreaming of tents, but because such were its origins; that unknown collective ancestry still cause fascination in Israel's present.

This application of the pastoral image in an unexpected context is not without consequence for the educational purpose Ben Sirach had in mind. By describing the divine pedagogy in pastoral terms, he is supplying a model for anyone who would undertake a formative activity in the community. It indicates an aspect that one should never lose sight of: the global and affectionate care of the person. Without a doubt, there is always the need to recall, correct and teach, but not as detached functions, as ends in themselves; rather, the aim is to restore unity, as the shepherd does with the flock.

Philo of Alexandria, the great philosopher of Jewish-Hellenist culture, has gathered and developed this idea applying the pastoral symbolism to the self-educative capacity of the individual. In every man there moves a small flock of emotions, of thoughts and desires. It is the task of reason (*Logos*, or Word) to lead them back to unity, and thereby exercise that function which Ben Sirach sees expressed in the mercy of the Creator.

We wish to conclude this examination with Ecclesiastes, although this writing is far more ancient than Ecclesiasticus (the precise date is questionable and can vary considerably from one scholar to another: from 500 BC, or even earlier, to circa 250 BC). The reason for this choice is that while Ecclesiasticus maintains the biblical tradition, Ecclesiastes occupies a place apart.

A common element in the two sapiential writings is the educational value of the term 'shepherd'. In Ecclesiasticus, however, the reflection revolves around the sign of mercy, in Ecclesiastes, under the sign of the spur.

If we wish to understand the meaning of the small phrase which interests us (Eccles 12:13), we must pause a while over this difficult and mysterious book.

The author bears a name which is a feminine participle derived from the word *qahal*, equivalent to the Greek *ekklesia* 'assembly' (from which comes our term 'church'). It should signify 'voice (or authority) that convokes' (in Greek *ekklesiastes*). He presents himself as 'son of David, king in Jerusalem' (Eccles

ECCLESIASTES
The words of the sages: given by one Shepherd

The small flock

Moses says, "Let the Lord, the God of the spirits and of all flesh, appoint a man over this congregation"; then, after adding a few words, he continues, "And the congregation of the Lord shall not be as sheep that have no shepherd" (Num 27:16f). Is it not well to pray that the flock linked to each one of us by a common birth and a common growth may not be left without a ruler and guide?

(Philo,
On Husbandry, §§44-45)

For when the protector, or governor, or father, or whatever we like to call him, of our complex being, namely right reason, has gone off leaving to itself the flock within us, the flock itself being left unattended perishes, and great loss is entailed upon its owner, while the irrational and unprotected creature, bereft of a guardian of the herd to admonish and discipline it, finds itself banished to a great distance from rational and immortal life.

(Philo, *The Posterity and Exile of Cain*, §68

There is a small flock in the heart of every person, a flock that is born and grows with us.

1:1), and thereby is identified with Solomon. But the scholars retain that this is a fictitious attribution resulting from the fact that Solomon was the founder and traditional patron of the wisdom of Israel.

However, a royal atmosphere, or nonetheless aristocratic, pervades the book: refined language, elevated disputes, research into all kinds of experiences, including the extravagant (Eccles 2:1-11). The sage essentially presents the fruits of his own personal experience, but he also understands the doctrine of the more ancient masters, as we shall see further on.

The Preacher is not a nihilist as might appear to be the case; on the contrary, he loves to savour the joys of life, which are gifts of God (Eccles 3:13). It could be said of him that he drinks life 'to the dregs', but immediately after, he affirms the lack of substance in the joy experienced (Eccles 2:11).

The biblical interpreters are used to presenting him as a wise man, critical of traditional doctrine. The Preacher would demonstrate, in practice, the contradictions met by the so-called 'dogma of retributions', which can be formulated in the following manner: whoever does good receives good, whoever does evil receives evil (from life, or from God). The Preacher would teach that, on the contrary, reality does not make distinctions between the good and the evil; it does not even differentiate between man and beast insofar as final destiny is concerned (Eccles 3:18-22). He therefore inculcates, after all, a '*carpe diem*' of ill-concealed pagan stamp (Eccles 5:17).

We claim that this judgment does not do justice to the biblical text. The Preacher does not mark the crisis nor the end of a traditional wisdom, infected by an dogged optimism. Certainly, his affirmations nearly always are in contrast with one another, radical affirmations alternated without shades of meaning. But the sense intended by the author is not found solely in the negative formulation, nor in the positive, but it is discovered by combining both in a sound balance.

To say that something is good and at the same time evil, does not signify for the Preacher affirming the nothingness of reality, nor supporting that it is guided by a blind destiny. On the contrary, he has a very strong sense of God and of his sovereignty. All things come from his hand and are 'the share' assigned to us (Eccles 3:22; 5:17). The point is that things are not placed at our disposal to be enjoyed or rejected as we please. There is a time both determined and variable, a time in which a thing is good, and a time in which the same thing is evil: 'there is a time to be born, and a time to die; a time to plant, and a time to pluck up what is planted... a time to weep, and a time to laugh... a time to embrace, and a time to refrain from embracing (Eccles 3:2-5).

71. HE TAUGHT THE PEOPLE WISDOM (Eccles 12:9)

Aramaean scribe with a pen pouch and a tablet of pliable wax. Detail from a relief from the palace of the Aramaean King Bar Rakab at Zingirli, Turkey (VIII century BC; Berlin National Museum).

This doctrine of the proper time is in no way the proclamation of a fixed destiny. It is rather a means by which he Preacher makes space (and ample space) for the liberty of God in our. We need to reflect on this for a moment. With the generalized norms that the wisdom of Israel continued to formulate (think, for example, of the sayings of Proverbs 10 and following chapters), the ancient wisdom of Israel could easily have grown false, 'dogmatic'. Since it was in the hands of people who did not have a lively awareness of God, of his freedom of action, and of the possibility at any moment of his direct intervention in the world.

We have an eloquent example in the doctrinal position defended by the three so-called friends of Job, who repeat, with little or no variation, the same doctrine. If Job has been stricken by a illness he 'must' have committed some sins, at least hidden or unconscious, because God 'must' reward whoever does good, he 'cannot' punish him.

It is against this dogmatic wisdom, that claims to determine the reaction of God to the behaviour of humanity – and that in practice wrongs both humanity and God – that the Preacher reacts to violently, almost blasphemously; his reaction is not against biblical wisdom in general.

What we have already said permits us to focus on a short text which interests us. It is contained in the epilogue of the composition, which gives a complex evaluation of the work of the Preacher:

> Besides being wise,
> the Preacher also taught the people knowledge,
> weighing and studying and arranging proverbs with great care.
> The Preacher sought to find pleasing words,
> and uprightly he wrote words of truth.
> The sayings of the wise are like goads,
> and like nails firmly fixed are the collected sayings
> which are given by one Shepherd (Eccles 12:9-11).

These phrases are surprising for various reasons. Modern interpreters are wont to say that they are a 'canonical' addition, intended, that is, somehow to 'baptize', a writing which at times seems blasphemous, and thus allow (or justify) its inclusion in the canon of inspired books. But if there is any truth in what we have said above, this conclusion is neither necessary nor convincing.

Various elements are important in the epilogue of Ecclesiastes; the expressions: 'words of truth' and 'words of the sages' (which literally recall Proverbs 22:21 and Proverbs 22:17); the term shepherd referred to God; and the image of the spur. Referring

72. THE SAYINGS OF THE WISE ARE GOADS (Eccles 12:11)

Egyptian limestone statuette from Thebes (VI century BC; Paris, Louvre Museum).

back to Proverbs, which is wisdom literature *par excellence*, the Preacher intentionally aligns himself with tradition and evaluates it positively. This fact is in line with what has been said above, that the Preacher does not criticize wisdom as such, but rather a myopic interpretation of wisdom. The use of the term 'shepherd' recalls Ecclesiasticus in two ways: the title is referred to God and is understood equally in terms of teaching, instruction and correction. What differs, however, is the content of the teaching: in Ecclesiasticus, it is the wonders of creation; in Ecclesiastes, the teaching of the sages.

This last comment warrants particular attention. By reason of their coming from God ("they have been given by the only Shepherd"), the sayings of the sages are inspired Scripture. We have, then, an extraordinary enrichment of the image: God is our shepherd not only because by contemplating creation we can see his pedagogic work (Ecclesiasticus), but also because he has given us the wise sayings of the sages. More generally, God is called 'Shepherd' in Ecclesiastes because he has given the Scriptures to humanity.

In place of the four verbs which specify the pastoral action of God (recalling, correcting, teaching, leading back, Ecclus 18:13),

---

The shepherd's goad

Rabbi Joshua gave this exposition: *The words of the wise are as goads, and as nails well fastened are the words of masters of assemblies* (Eccles 12:11): as the goad guides the heifer along its furrows, so do the words of the Torah guide a man along the paths of life...

Masters of assemblies: these are the disciples of the wise who enter (the house of study) and sit in several groups; some declare a thing forbidden others declaring it permitted, some pronounce a thing unclean others pronouncing it clean, some rule a thing unfit others ruling it fit.

Now lest a man say to you, "I will sit idle and not study", the text continues, *They are given from one shepherd*: i.e. one God created them, one leader gave them, the Lord of all creation uttered them.

Therefore make your ear like a funnel and allow to enter therein the words of those who forbid and those who permit, the words of those who pronounce unclean and of those who pronounce clean, the words of those who rule it unfit and of those who rule it fit".

(*Abot* de Rabbi Natan 18:2)

Make your ear like a funnel, let enter the words of the wise! They come from the divine shepherd and carry one on the road of life.

the Preacher uses the image of the spur, that is, the instrument used by the farmer to direct and goad his animals; as well as that of 'well-planted nails'. The sense of the second image is not clear; it could add to the preceding one (nails planted in the spur), or rather, suggest the idea of stability (as the tent-peg planted in solid ground, see Isaiah 22:23).

The image of the spur is easily understood in the light of what has already been said on the style of the Preacher and his reasoning in strong contrasts. The sayings of the sages are a sharp pain that the spur of the shepherd inflicts on humanity to save them from becoming complacent and self-righteous, and even from the false security of believing that reality proceeds in foreseeable directions. It seeks to be a reminder that, on the contrary, reality is manifold and variable; it is not contradictory and self-destructive only because God sustains it and gives it meaning.

Humanity, therefore, must remain watchful and alert. They may find enjoyment in things, but at the same time they must be conscious of their emptiness. They may dedicate themselves to achieving their goals, but without exaggeration. In a word, behind every event, joyful or otherwise, they must discover the face of the one and only Shepherd, if they wants to penetrate the meaning of life, the ultimate sense of a wonderful and a fleeting reality.

Conclusions and Perspectives

We have flown over the world of pastoral symbolism in the Bible, from the *Torah* to the Prophets, from the Psalms to Ecclesiastes. In this flight at low altitude, we have observed in all its beauty a meaningful panorama, made up of both simple and complex elements. An ancient environment, sculpted, as it were, by the passing of the ages, yet still palpitating and capable of vibrating with new life.

From the banks of the Mesopotamian rivers to those of the Nile, we have followed in the footsteps of the patriarchs, continuously pulling up tent pegs and moving on again towards new horizons. The needs of his offspring oblige Jacob to flee and face up to the rigours of an alien existence. Hunger forces Israel to fold up their tents and depart for Egypt, where they at first experience welcome, then tyranny and finally liberation at the hand of a Moses who is misunderstood by his own brothers and forced to escape from them to live as an alien. Even David, the consecrated leader of Israel, is reduced to a vagrant lifestyle before ascending to the throne, as if to experience for himself that confidence in the divine Shepherd which he teaches others to sing (Ps 23).

In this journey of ours, under the banner of biblical pastoral symbolism, we have uncovered aspects of rare beauty, feminine as well as masculine. There is Rachel, the shepherdess, beloved woman, mother who dies giving life, and through whose merits – the Rabbis comment – God leads Israel back from exile. There is Miriam, the sister who keeps watch over Moses, the prophetess who leads the people in dance, and intones the song of freedom; the woman who together with the man contributes to the rising up of the Waters of life from the deep well of the Torah. And there is Abigail, courageous and enterprising, who grasps the opportune moment to act with wisdom, freeing David from pretexts of wounded pride and from the blind logic of revenge.

Entering into the area of prophetic utterance and of the poetry of Israel, we have found ourselves confronted by a galaxy of symbols. Various images revolve around the pastoral symbolism: some by natural affinity, such as the staff and the tent; others by contrast, such as the threatening shadow of robbers and brigands and the roaring of wild beasts.

They are images which describe in an involving manner the relationship between God and Israel, even to the extent of boldness. We see a God who transforms himself from shepherd to wild beast and attacks the object of his love (Hosea); a God who is prepared to tear his people apart in order to save a remnant (Amos).

The prophets weave contrasting images that cannot easily be contained within the rigid parameters of theology, as if to indicate that God transcends all our utterance: he is goodness, but equally justice; he is holiness, but at the same time mercy toward sinners. Hence the figure of the warrior-king, who opens the breach and marches at the head of his people, is interwoven with that of the shepherd who stoops down to dress the wounds of his sheep (Micah, Second Isaiah and Zephaniah).

Without a doubt, God pronounces judgement against the leaders responsible for the scattering of the flock (Jeremiah, Ezekiel), but neither are the sheep absolved from their personal responsibility: they are included in the judgement. The shepherd of Israel will not allow himself to be deceived: he will go in search of the lost sheep and will raise up a new David to rule them.

Finally, we have seen how the pastoral symbolism accompanies the very prayer of the people of God, nurturing them with sentiments of gratitude and trust. The memory of the great deeds accomplished by the Lord in favour of Israel sustains hope in the moment of trial and teaches them to pray in every situation. Such is the relationship of love between God and Israel that poetry cannot cease to sing his praises: like a garden of a thousand blossoms and perfumes where he and she meet together, like the tents of the shepherds to which she leads her flock in order to meet her beloved (Song of Songs), like a spur that gives no respite (Ecclesiastes).

What can all this say to the Church of our day? I will briefly address three basic perspectives: the dimension of the laity, the art of governing and the wisdom exercised in pastoral care.

The dimension of the laity

One of the first conclusions that comes to light at the end of this work is precisely the dimension of the laity in the exercise of pastoral biblical care. This is not in the contemporary sense of our culture, but in the original sense of the term ('lay' derives from *laos*, meaning people), which is after all the biblical meaning. The patriarch and the matriarch, the leader who educates

163

the people and the prophetess, the king and the wise woman: these are the basic figures underlying the pastoral symbolism. In contrast, there is nothing to indicate (except indirectly) that the priests or Levites are seen as pastors. Pastoral care in the Old Testament and in the Judaic tradition is not a prerogative of the clergy, but of the laity.

This aspect stimulates us to reconsider the fundamental vocation of all the people of God, freeing the contemporary dimension of pastoral care from the strictures of clericalism to bring it out into the open arena of history, where the fundamental values of the family and of society come into play.

In the area of worship, the biblical figures we have been examining are also active. In certain instances they exercise a priestly rôle: for example, Jacob's behaviour at Bethel; the rôle of Moses at the consecration of Aaron; and David's performance when the ark is brought to Jerusalem. Nevertheless, the pastoral symbolism essentially favours secular circumstances. It is not the temple that comes first, but rather the people and the land that receives them. And before that, there is the descent of God into history, as seen in the life of Jacob and the experience of the exodus.

God pitches his tent in the midst of Israel and goes ahead of his people towards the promised land. Even when he dwells in a sanctuary made of stone, the presence of God is not fixed and bound to the temple. It is free and mobile: it moves away and returns, it precedes and follows the wandering of the people, even in exile, remaining the centre of cohesion and reason for hope.

The God of the Bible is the God of history not because he controls from above the unfolding of human events, but because he enters into human history and pitches his tent among his people. Consequently, it is on the grounds of history that Israel must learn to acknowledge its God as the only Lord and to render him the worship of obedience and love.

In this sense, every believer is called to exercise a pastoral rôle in the area of their own responsibilities: the father and mother in the context of the family; the teacher in the environment of the school; the politician in the difficult task of governing the *polis*, so that the state might not become a jungle dominated by the law of the strongest or of the most shrewd, but rather a nation founded on justice and the search for the common good.

The art of governing

The biblical tradition has used the figure of the shepherd to illustrate the ministry of one who is appointed as leader of the community. Above all, the figure of David has exercised a notable influence on the ecclesiastical tradition, where the pastoral function has been almost identified with the authority and the power of governing (*potestas regiminis*). The union between pastoral care and authority is well symbolized in the pastoral staff that is given to the bishop during the rite of ordination, and the meaning of which is, in fact, a pastoral form of authority.

Demonstrating a greater sensitivity for the lay connotation of the pastoral function in the Bible, the Second Vatican Council has brought to light the royal rôle of all the baptized (*Lumen Gentium*, 10 and 31). The community as well as the ecclesiastical hierarchy are gifted with the royal function. In his first encyclical, *Redemptor Hominis*, John Paul II has taken up and clarified the significance of this function, interpreting it essentially as service:

> In building up from the very foundations the picture of the Church as the People of God – by showing the threefold mission of Christ himself, through participation in which we become truly God's People – the Second Vatican Council highlighted, among other characteristics of the Christian vocation, the one that can be described as 'kingly'. (...) This dignity is expressed in readiness to serve, in keeping with the example of Christ, who "came not to be served but to serve" (Mt 20:28). If, in the light of this attitude of Christ's, 'being a king' is truly possible only by 'being a servant', then 'being a servant' also demands so much spiritual maturity that it must really be described as 'being a king'. In order to be able to serve others worthily and effectively we must be able to master ourselves, possess the virtues that make this mastery possible. Our sharing in Christ's kingly mission – his 'kingly function' (*munus*) – is closely linked with every sphere of both Christian and human morality (*Redemptor Hominis* 21)

At first sight, this excerpt could appear a very intimate one and devoid of political relevance. But this is not the case. Already Philo had discerned a close connection between the office of royalty and self-mastery and had expressed this relationship by using the figure of the shepherd. Those who are called to 'guide' others (whether spiritually or politically) must first see to their own direction, since it is only in a situation of self-control that they can enter into relationships with others in an exchange that does not lead to exploitation, but to service. In the exercise of the royal office in this way, there is the experience of an unbreakable bond between authority and service: not a power that humiliates, but a crucified royalty like that of Jesus, the good shepherd.

Pastoral wisdom

The power 'to govern' given to the Christian community requires that it seeks, in so far as possible, to guide the created world and the course of events wisely, so that they may reach their ultimate goal, Christ the Lord. For, the faithful "are called by God that, being led by the spirit to the Gospel, they may contribute to the sanctification of the world, as from within like leaven, by fulfilling their own particular duties" (*Lumen Gentium* 31).

It is a perspective of vast dimensions which usually becomes concrete in the humble areas of daily living. In this context, Christian authority from that of the hierarchy to that of the religious superior or of the father and mother of a family, should take on the characteristics of a pastoral style of government: a style that is not merely an accessory or ornament, but rather expresses a profound and essential connotation.

The model for the wise leader is the attitude of the shepherd towards his flock: of a flock that consists not only of sheep but also of people. In this concept resides the force of the imagery and its power to point to ever new horizons.

Revisiting the origins in this way is like drinking waters from a spring. One can draw inspiration to invent a pastoral care that is wise, adapted to the times and capable of utopia. In fact, the wisdom of good government is not merely expressed in preserving the values of the past, but in the capacity to shift the tent of human society towards new frontiers.

73. I WILL SURELY GATHER ALL
  OF YOU, O JACOB
  (Mic 2:12)

Detail of an Egyptian limestone relief from the tomb of Ti at Saqqara, Egypt; 2400 BC.

The biblical pastoral dimension unleashes a mighty current of utopia. It is not to be found in taking the world back to the nomadic condition of the patriarchs, but in moving it onwards towards that tent which will be forever the dwelling-place of God amongst humanity, when the Lamb will lead the redeemed to the springs of life and the Father will wipe away every tear from our eyes (cf Rev 7:17).

To that final goal, men and women are called to travel together, recounting their faith experiences in the daily fabric of history. Together they are called to cause the waters of wisdom to rise up from the deep well of the Word of God, for the benefit of new generations, and to guide the flock entrusted to them by the supreme shepherd to living pastures, transforming each point of arrival into new departures.

GLOSSARY OF HEBREW TERMS

ABOT (*Pirke Abot*), 'Sayings of the Fathers'. This is a Mishnaic treatise in six chapters, which gathers together the opinions of eminent rabbis. It is considered to be the highest expression of the religious ethics of Judaism. It has a priviliged position, as it is used in the Synagogue liturgy.

ABOT de Rabbi Natan, 'The Fathers of Rabbi Natan'. A 'minor' treatise of the *Talmud*, containing many traditions parallel to those in the Mishnaic *Pirke Abot*.

AGGADAH (or *haggadah*, pl. *haggadot*), 'account'. It derives from the root *nagad*, meaning 'to relate, to give an account'. Hence, it refers to one of the most characteristic literary genres of Judaism. The *aggadah* relates the text of the Bible using many images and anecdotes borrowed from both popular tradition and profound spirituality. Particularly famous is the *Aggadah of the Passover* about the liberation from Egypt: it contains prayers and hymns adapted to the celebration of the rite. From thirteenth century onwards, highly decorative *haggadot* were produced for use by families.

'AM, 'people'. The term is very often used to refer specifically to Israel as a 'chosen people' as separate from the *goyim* ('pagan nations, peoples'). In the Psalms, *'am* is frequently associated with pastoral imagery (e.g. 'the people of your flock').

AMORA (pl. *amoraim*), 'interpreter(s)'. It derives from the root *'amar*, meaning 'to say, to interpret'. The scholars of the Scriptures who lived between 200 and 600 AD – the period between the redaction of the *Mishnah* and the end of the Talmudic era – are called 'Amorei'.

GER (pl. *gerim*), 'foreigner(s), stranger(s)'. In the first place, the term points to the nomadic condition of Moses and the patriarchs. Later, it refers to resident foreigners in Jewish territory. The Septuagint translates *ger* by *proselytos* ('proselyte'), thus introducing a religious connotation referring to the foreigner who converted to Judaism.

YHWH, 'Yahweh'. This is the four-lettered abbreviation for the divine name, as revealed to Moses on Mount Sinai. Out of a very real sense of respect for the divine name, Judaism avoids pronouncing it. So, when a biblical text is read, *Adonai* 'my Lord' is used to replace it, pronounced as determined by the Masoretes.

MEKILTA, 'rule, measure, legal norm'. An exegetical *Midrash* up until the Exodus, in which interpretations of ethical characters (*halaka*) rather than haggadic accounts are predominant.

MEMAR MARQAH, 'Teaching of Marqah'. A Samaritan *Targum* containing an anthology of ancient traditions from north Israel, dating from the second to the fourth century AD.

MIDRASH (pl. *midrashim*), 'investigation, research'. The term derives from *darash*, 'to search, to investigate'. It refers first of all to the exegetical method which was typical of the rabbinical tradition: analysis of all the particulars of a text, even the apparently not so significant elements, so as to draw out the hidden meaning. It is necessary to search for the profound meaning which is not immediately obvious. Later, it refers to the written results of this investigation. The great midrashic compilations contain verse by verse explanations of the various books of the Bible.

MIDRASH HAGGADOL, 'The great Midrash'. This is the commentary on the Pentateuch which uses traditional material. It was edited in the twelfth century AD.

MIDRASH RABBAH, 'great Midrash'. A collection of the superior rabbinic interpretations of the Pentateuch and the five *Meghillot* 'scrolls', viz. Song of Songs, Ruth, Lamentations, Ecclesiastes and Esther.

MIDRASH TEHILLIM, 'Midrash of the Psalms'. This contains material from different ages, some as old as the third century AD. It was edited some time between 900 and 1100 AD.

NAGID, 'leader, chief'. In its most ancient sense, it referred to the leader of flocks. Only later, by extension, was it used to refer to the one who guided the people. The correlation between the task of shepherding and the title of *nagid* comes across especially in the story of David.

PESIKTA RABBATI, 'great part (chapter)'. A homiletic *Midrash* on texts concerning feasts and the Sabbath. It was edited in the sixth to the seventh century AD, but contains some older material.

PIRKE, 'chapters', of RABBI ELIEZER. This is a narrative *Midrash* of the Pentateuch in 54 chapters, and edited in the nineth to the tenth century AD.

RO'EH (fem. *ro'ah*), 'shepherd, shepherdess': the substantive participle of the verb *ra'ah*, meaning 'to graze, to look after the flock'.

SEGULLAH, 'property'. This term refers to the specific relationship of intimacy and belonging which bound Israel to her God.

SHEKINAH, 'residence (of God)'. This points to the presence of God in the sanctuary, in the community, or in each individual Jew. Some texts affirm that the *shekinah* was withdrawn from Israel with the destruction of the first temple; others maintain that it went with Israel into exile; others again hold that it is present in the community at prayer.

SHOMER, 'guard', from the root *shamar*, meaning 'to guard'. It referred both to the sentry who guarded the city, and the shepherd, the 'guard of the flock'.

SIFRE, 'books'. A tannaite *Midrash* on Numbers and Deuteronomy, of predominantly halakhic content; it dates from perhaps the third century AD.

SUKKAH (pl. *Sukkot*), 'hut(s)'. The term designates the feast of huts (or of the Tabernacles) which begins on fifteenth of the month of Tishri (between September and October) and recalls the 40 years of wandering in the desert, when Israel lived in tents. Even today, during the seven days of the feast, Jews reside in huts.

TALMUD, 'teaching, study'. This incorporates the *Mishnah* 'repetition, teaching', an edition of the oral tradition regarding religious legislation (second century AD), and a *Mishnah* commentary called *Gemarah* ('complement' of the *Mishnah*). It is a weighty collection, gathering together the opinions and discussions of the Amorei scholars (cf *Amora*). There are two versions: the *Palestinian Talmud*, or Jerusalem Talmud, was edited between the fourth and the fifth century AD, and is in Hebrew and Palestinian Aramaic. The *Babylonian Talmud* was composed between V and VI century AD in the Babylonian schools, and is in Hebrew and Babylonian Aramaic. The latter, being the more extensive and prestigious, was recognized as canonical, and from the eleventh century until the present day it has become 'the' *Talmud*.

TANNA (pl. *tannaim*), 'teacher, repeater'. It comes from the Aramaic *tanah*, 'to repeat, to learn'. The teachers who taught from 10 to 220 AD and started the *Mishnah* are known as Tannaites. They are given the title of 'rabbis'.

TANNA DEBE ELIJJAHU, 'The teacher of the school of Elijah'. A relatively autonomous Midrashic work, differing from all the other *midrashim* in that it is not a commentary on a biblical text, but an autonomous instructive composition.

TARGUM (pl. *targumin*), 'translation': from the verb *tirgem*, 'to translate, to explain'. After the exile, it was felt necessary to translate into the Aramaic of the assembly those parts of Scripture which were read in Hebrew. The translation was not so literal, so the text was expanded and made topical, and enriched by many paraphrases. The *Targumin* were closely connected with the Synagogue liturgy. The ones we know of are: *Targum of the Pentateuch* (*Onkelos, Neophyte*); *Jerushalmi I* or *Pseudo-Jonathan Targum*; *Fragmentary* or *Jerushalmi II Targum*; *Targum of the Prophets*; *Targum of the Hagiographies*.

TORAH, 'teaching, law'. The term is derived from the root *yarah*, 'to teach'; in its technical sense, it refers to the Pentateuch.

TSO'N, 'flock' of small livestock (sheep or goats).

BIBLIOGRAPHY

Egyptian and Mesopotamian texts:

Bosetti E., *La terminologia del pastore in Egitto e nella Bibbia* in *Bibbia e Oriente* 140 (1984) 75-102.

Donadoni S., *Testi religiosi egizi*, Torino 1970.

Pritchard J.B., *Ancient Near Eastern texts relating to the Old Testament*, Princeton 1969.

Seux M.J., *Hymnes et prières aux dieux de Babylone et d'Assyrie*, Paris 1976.

Vorlander H., *Mein Gott*, Kevelaer/Neukirchen 1975.

Jewish texts:

Bietenhard H., *Sifre Deuteronomium*, Bern 1984.

Bietenhard H., *Midrash Tanhuma: R. Tanhuma über die Tora, genannt Midrash Jelammedenu*, I-II, Bern 1980-82.

Braude W.G., *Pesikta Rabbati: discourses for feasts, fasts, and special sabbaths*, I-II, Yale 1968.

Braude W.G., *The Midrash on the Psalms*, I-II. New Haven 1959.

Braude W.G. and Kapstein I.J., *Tanna Debe Elijjahu: The lore of the school of Elijah*, Philadelphia 1981.

Charlesworth J.C., *The Old Testament pseudepigrapha*, 1-2, London 1983-85.

Cohen A., ed., *The minor tractates of the Talmud*, I-II, London 1971.

Colson F.H. and Whitaker G.H., *Philo*, II-III, London 1968.

Diez Macho A., *Neophites 1. Palestinian Targum, manuscripts of the Vatican library, I, Génesis*, Madrid-Barcelona 1968.

Epstein I., *The Babylonian Talmud*, London 1935-52.

Freedmann H. and Simon M., *Midrash Rabbah: translated into English with notes, glossary and indices*, I-X, 3 ed., London 1961.

Friedlander G., *Pirke of Rabbi Eliezer: the chapters of Rabbi Eliezer the Great*, 4 ed., New York 1981.

Ginzberg L., *The legends of the Jews*, I-VII. Philadelphia 1968.

Kasher M.M., *Torah Shelemah, Genesis*, VII, New York l950.

Lauterbach J.Z., *Mekilta of Rabbi Ishmael*, 1-3, Philadelphia 1933-35.

Le Déaut R., *Miriam, soeur de Moïse, et Marie, Mère du Messie* in *Biblica* 45 (1964) 198-219.

Le Déaut R., *Targum du Pentateuque*, I-II, Paris 1978-1979.

Lewin B.M. and Epstein A., *Yalqut Shim'oni*, I-II, Jerusalem 1967.

MacDonald J., *Marqah: Memar Marqah, the teaching of Marqah*, I-II, Berlin 1963.

McNamara M., *Targum Neofiti 1: Genesis, translated with apparatus and notes*, Edinburgh 1992.

Navarro Peiro M.A., *Abot de Rabbi Natan*, Institución S. Jerónimo para la investigación bíblica, Valencia 1987.

Pritchard J.B., *Ancient Near Eastern texts relating to the Old Testament*, Princeton 1969.

Rabinowitz Z.M., *Midrash Haggadot on the Pentateuch. Edited from various manuscripts with introduction*, 4 ed., Jerusalem 1983.

Silbermann A.M. in coll. with Rosenbaum M., *Chumas with Targum Onkelos, Haphtaroth and Rashi's commentary*, Jerusalem 1985.